I0479126

9 to 5:

Unethical Behaviour Discouraged

By Max Hunter

Copyright © 2023 All rights reserved.

Paperback ISBN: 9798391593386
Hardcover ISBN: 9798391598572

Why You Shouldn't Treat Your Job Like a Nap Time: And Other Lessons From Kindergarten

How to Make Your Boss Laugh: A Guide to Productivity Through Humour

Zen and the Art of Procrastination: The Art of Doing Nothing... Productively

Don't Let Your Desk Become a Black Hole: The Art of Organization

Why Your Co-workers Aren't Mind Readers: Effective Communication Strategies in the Workplace

How to Survive a Meeting Without Falling Asleep: The Ultimate Guide to Staying Awake

Why Multi-Tasking is Overrated: The Art of Single-Tasking for Increased Productivity"

Dealing With Difficult Co-workers: A Survival Guide

Why You Should Embrace Feedback (Even When It Hurts): The Importance of Constructive Criticism

Why You Should Never Hit 'Reply All': Email Etiquette in the Workplace

The Power of Positive Thinking (And Positive People): How Your Attitude Affects Your Work

Why You Shouldn't Be a Lone Wolf: The Importance of Teamwork in the Workplace

How to Deal With an Overbearing Boss: A Guide to Navigating Difficult Relationships

Why Your Office Needs a Pet: The Benefits of Workplace Animals

How to Win Friends and Influence Co-workers: The Art of Networking

Why a Clean Office is a Productive Office: The Importance of Cleanliness

How to Be Assertive Without Being Aggressive: Standing Up for Yourself in the Workplace

Why Work/Life Balance is Essential: The Art of Taking Time Off

Why You Should Always Be Learning: The Importance of Professional Development

Why a Sense of Humour is the Best Tool in Your Work Toolbox: Laughter in the Workplace

How to Deal With a Micromanaging Boss: A Guide to Keeping Your Sanity

Why You Shouldn't Fear Failure: Learning From Mistakes in the Workplace

The Benefits of Exercise at Work: How Physical Activity Can Improve Your Workday

Why You Shouldn't Be Afraid to Ask for Help: The Power of Collaboration

The Secret to Success: The Importance of Persistence in the Workplace

Are you tired of the same old routine at work? Do you feel like you're just going through the motions without any real joy or excitement? It's time to inject some fun back into your work life!

Work doesn't have to be a drag. In fact, adding a little bit of fun to your daily tasks can actually increase productivity, creativity, and overall job satisfaction. But how do you do that? That's where this book comes in.

We've all heard the phrase "work hard, play hard," but how often do we actually put that into practice? It's time to change that. This book is here to help you discover the benefits of incorporating fun into your work life and provide you with practical ways to do it.

But wait, you might be thinking, "isn't work supposed to be serious?" While there are certainly times when seriousness is required, that doesn't mean you can't have a little fun along the way. In fact, studies have shown that employees who have fun at work are more engaged, have higher job satisfaction, and are more likely to stay with their company long-term.

So, what are some ways to add some fun into your work life? How about starting a weekly office game night, having a themed potluck, or setting up a team-building activity? These are just a few examples of how you can inject some fun into your workday.

But it's not just about the activities you do. It's also about the attitude you bring to work. By approaching your work with a positive and playful attitude, you can make even the most mundane tasks enjoyable. Plus, having a positive attitude can also help boost morale among your co-workers, making for a more enjoyable work environment overall.

But don't just take our word for it. Give it a try for yourself! Start small by incorporating one fun activity into your workday and see how it affects your productivity and overall job satisfaction. We guarantee you'll be pleasantly surprised.

So, what are you waiting for? It's time to put the fun back in your work life and start reaping the benefits. Let's work hard and play hard together!

Why You Shouldn't Treat Your Job Like a Nap Time: And Other Lessons From Kindergarten

Have you ever heard the phrase "Work Hard, Play Hard?" It's a phrase that emphasizes the importance of balancing hard work with fun and relaxation. Unfortunately, some people take this phrase to mean that they can treat their job like nap time and still get paid. But the truth is, treating your job like nap time is not only unprofessional, but it can also hurt your career in the long run.

In fact, there are several lessons we learned in kindergarten that are still relevant in the workplace today. One of the most important lessons is the value of hard work. In kindergarten, we learned that we had to work hard to learn new things and accomplish tasks. We had to practice our letters and numbers, follow directions, and clean up after ourselves. These lessons taught us that hard work is necessary to succeed.

The same lesson applies to the workplace. If you want to succeed in your job, you need to work hard. This means showing up on time, being prepared, and giving your best effort. If you treat your job like nap time, you're not putting in the effort required to succeed.

Another lesson we learned in kindergarten is the importance of following rules. In kindergarten, we had rules for everything. We had to raise our hands to speak, line up in single file, and use inside voices. These rules taught us to respect authority and follow procedures.

In the workplace, there are rules and procedures that must be followed as well. This could include dress codes, safety regulations, or company policies. If you treat your job like nap time, you may be more likely to break these rules, which could lead to disciplinary action or even termination.

A third lesson we learned in kindergarten is the importance of being respectful. In kindergarten, we learned to be kind to others, share our toys, and listen when others are speaking. These lessons taught us to be respectful of others' feelings and opinions.

In the workplace, being respectful is just as important. This means treating co-workers and customers with kindness and understanding. If you treat your job like nap time, you may be more likely to be rude or dismissive of others, which could damage your professional reputation.

Finally, in kindergarten, we learned the importance of taking responsibility for our actions. If we broke a toy or spilled our milk, we had to clean it up and apologize. These lessons taught us that we are responsible for our own actions and mistakes.

In the workplace, taking responsibility is crucial. This means owning up to mistakes and taking steps to correct them. If you treat your job like nap time, you may be more likely to blame others for your mistakes, which could damage your professional relationships.

So, why shouldn't you treat your job like nap time? Because doing so can hurt your career in the long run. By ignoring the lessons we learned in kindergarten, you risk being seen as unprofessional, disrespectful, and unreliable. If you want to succeed in your job, you need to work hard, follow the rules, be respectful, and take responsibility for your actions. By doing so, you'll not only improve your professional reputation, but you'll also increase your chances of success in the workplace.

In conclusion, the lessons we learned in kindergarten are still relevant in the workplace today. By working hard, following the rules, being respectful, and taking responsibility for our actions, we can improve our chances of success in the workplace. So, the next time you're tempted to treat your job like nap time, remember the lessons you learned in kindergarten and put in the effort required to succeed.

How to Make Your Boss Laugh: A Guide to Productivity Through Humour

We all know that work can be stressful, but did you know that injecting some humour into your day can actually increase productivity? That's right, making your boss laugh can not only lighten the mood, but it can also help you get more done. Here's a guide to using humour to boost productivity in the workplace.

Know your audience.

You know how everyone's got their own sense of humour, right? What makes one person laugh might make another person cringe. So, if you're going to try to crack a joke, it's super important to know who you're talking to.

Let's say you're trying to impress your boss with your witty banter. You got to be careful not to offend them, or worse, get yourself fired. So, pay attention to what kind of humour they like. Do they like cheesy puns or sarcastic remarks? Are they into dry humour or slapstick comedy? Figure out their style, and then tailor your jokes to match.

And if you're not sure what kind of humour your boss is into, don't worry. Start with something safe, like a classic dad joke or a silly observation about something in the room. If they don't laugh, no harm done. At least you didn't risk offending them.

Remember, humour is a powerful tool. It can break the ice, lighten the mood, and even make you more likable. But it can also backfire if you're not careful. So, be mindful of your audience, and always aim to make them smile, not cringe.

Keep it appropriate.

We all know that cracking a joke can ease the tension and make work more bearable. But, there are some jokes that are a big no-no in the workplace.

For instance, anything that's sexist, racist, or just plain offensive should be avoided like the plague. You don't want to risk making your boss or their colleagues feel uncomfortable or insulted. That's just asking for trouble!

The key is to keep it appropriate, people. You don't have to be a total buzzkill, but think before you speak. Ask yourself, "Could this joke offend someone?" If the answer is yes, then maybe save it for happy hour with your friends instead.

Remember, your goal is to make your boss laugh, not tick them off. So, be mindful of your words and actions in the workplace. You don't want to ruin your reputation or get yourself in hot water over a silly joke. Play it safe, and save the edgy humour for outside of work.

Use self-deprecating humour.

You know, making fun of yourself to get a few laughs? It can be a real ice-breaker, especially with your boss.

For instance, you could poke fun at your own forgetfulness or clumsiness. Maybe you spilled coffee on your shirt this morning or forgot your own name in the meeting. You can turn that into a joke, and show your boss that you're not taking yourself too seriously.

But, you got to be careful not to overdo it. You don't want to come across as too negative or insecure. Self-deprecating humour is all about laughing at yourself, not beating yourself up. So, keep it light and don't go too hard on yourself.

Remember, humour is a powerful tool in the workplace. It can make you more likable, and help you build better relationships with your colleagues and boss. But, use it wisely, and don't take it too far. Self-deprecating humour can be hilarious, but don't let it turn into self-sabotage.

Use humour to diffuse tension.

You know how things can get real tense when there's a disagreement between co-workers? That's where a little bit of humour can go a long way.

For instance, you could crack a joke to lighten the mood and take the edge off. Maybe it's a witty one-liner or a funny observation about the situation. The point is to make people laugh and help them relax a bit.

But listen up. You got to be careful with your humour, especially in sensitive situations. Don't make light of the disagreement or belittle anyone involved. And, definitely don't use humour to offend or insult anyone. That's just going to make things worse.

The key is to use humour to diffuse tension, not add to it. So, think before you speak, and make sure your joke is appropriate for the situation. If in doubt, go with something light-hearted and silly.

Remember, humour can be a powerful tool in the workplace. But use it wisely and with good intentions. A well-timed joke can bring people together and make work more bearable.

Use humour to boost creativity.

Do you know when you're having a good laugh and feeling relaxed? Well, that's when your brain is most open to new ideas and thinking outside the box.

That's why it's a great idea to inject a bit of humour into brainstorming sessions and meetings with your team. Encourage everyone to let loose and have some fun. Crack a joke or two, and watch as the creative juices start flowing.

When you're in a relaxed state of mind, you're more likely to come up with innovative ideas that you might not have thought of otherwise. Plus, a bit of humour can make the whole process more enjoyable and less stressful.

But, don't go too crazy with the humour. You don't want to waste too much time joking around and not actually getting any work done. Just keep it light and fun, and see where the creativity takes you.

So, go ahead and have some laughs with your team. You might just be surprised by what you come up with.

Use humour to build relationships.

Did you know that humour can help you build stronger relationships with your boss and colleagues? It's true! When you share a good laugh with someone, you're more likely to feel relaxed and comfortable around them. And that's a great foundation for effective teamwork.

So, don't be afraid to inject a bit of humour into your work relationships. Crack a joke or two, or share a funny story. It'll help you connect with your co-workers on a more personal level, and build a sense of camaraderie.

But listen up. You can't just use humour to avoid serious conversations or brush off important issues. That's not going to fly. You got to be willing to tackle tough topics head-on, even if it's uncomfortable.

That being said, humour can be a great tool to help diffuse tension and bring people together. Just make sure you're using it appropriately, and not as a way to avoid the hard stuff.

So, go ahead and have some laughs with your boss and colleagues. It'll make work more enjoyable and help you build better relationships. Just remember to balance it out with serious discussions when needed.

Don't force it.

You know how some people just aren't naturally funny? Well, that's totally okay! You don't have to force humour in the workplace.

If you're not the type to crack jokes or make others laugh, don't try to be someone you're not. Your boss and colleagues will appreciate your genuine personality more than a cringe-worthy attempt at humour. Trust me on this one.

Now, if you do want to inject some humour into your work life, that's cool too. But, make sure you're doing it in a way that feels natural to you. Don't force jokes or try too hard to be funny. It'll just come off as awkward and uncomfortable for everyone involved.

And, if you're not sure if something is actually funny, bounce it off a trusted colleague or friend first. They'll give you an honest opinion and help you avoid any potential workplace faux pas.

So, to sum it up, be yourself and don't force humour. If it comes naturally to you, go for it! But, if not, don't stress about it. Just be your awesome self and let your personality shine through.

In conclusion, humour can be a powerful tool in the workplace. By using it appropriately and knowing your audience, you can make your boss laugh and boost productivity at the same time. Whether it's using self-deprecating humour, diffusing tension, boosting creativity, building relationships, or simply making a silly observation, injecting some humour into your day can make work more enjoyable and effective. So, don't be afraid to let your funny side shine and see how it can benefit you and your team.

Zen and the Art of Procrastination: The Art of Doing Nothing... Productively

Procrastination is often viewed as a negative habit. We're told that we should always be productive, and that if we're not doing something, we're wasting time. But what if there was a way to turn procrastination into a productive habit? What if we could use our natural inclination towards doing nothing to actually get more done? That's where the idea of "Zen and the Art of Procrastination" comes in.

The idea of "Zen" has long been associated with a state of mind where we are fully present and focused on the task at hand. It's a state of mind where we are calm, centred, and in control. Procrastination, on the other hand, is often associated with distraction, avoidance, and lack of focus. But what if we could merge these two seemingly opposite states of mind to create something new?

The key to this concept is to recognize that procrastination is not always a bad thing. It can be a way for our minds to take a break and recharge before tackling a big project. Sometimes, we need to step away from a task to gain a fresh perspective, and that's where "Zen procrastination" comes in. Here are some tips for how to make procrastination work for you:

Embrace the pause.

Instead of beating yourself up for not being productive, try seeing it as an opportunity to take a break and re-center yourself. Take a few moments to clear your mind, breathe deeply, and focus on the present moment. It can help you approach your work with a fresh perspective and renewed energy.

Sometimes, when we're too focused on getting things done, we forget to take care of ourselves. And that can lead to burnout and a lack of motivation. So, if you find yourself procrastinating, don't stress about it. Take a step back and give yourself a chance to recharge.

Of course, you can't procrastinate forever. At some point, you got to buckle down and get to work. But, taking a little break every now and then can actually help you be more productive in the long run. So, don't beat yourself up for procrastinating. Embrace it as an opportunity to reset and recharge, and you'll be back on track in no time!

Set intentions.

When you decide to take a breather, be intentional about it. Have a plan for what you want to do during your break. Maybe you want to do a quick meditation, go for a walk in the park to clear your head, or even just read a chapter of your favourite book. Whatever it is, make sure it's something that'll help you recharge and refresh.

By setting an intention for your break, you're making it more purposeful and productive. You'll come back to your work with a clearer head and renewed energy. Plus, you'll feel good about actually accomplishing something during your break.

So, the next time you need to take a break, take a moment to think about what you want to do. Don't just go through the motions - be intentional and make it count!

Do nothing...on purpose.

Sometimes, when you're feeling overwhelmed or drained, the best way to recharge is to just sit and be present. Take a few minutes to observe your thoughts and feelings without judgement. Don't try to suppress them or analyse them - just let them be.

Believe it or not, this can actually help you gain clarity and perspective. It's like hitting the reset button on your brain. After a few minutes of doing nothing, you'll be able to approach your work with a clearer mind and a fresh perspective.

So, the next time you're feeling burnt out, try taking a few minutes to do nothing. It might seem counterintuitive but trust me - it really works!

Break up big tasks.

So, do you know that feeling when you have a huge project looming over you and you just don't know where to start? Yeah, it's the worst. But don't worry - I've got a tip that might help.

Instead of trying to tackle the whole thing at once, try breaking it up into smaller, more manageable tasks. This way, you won't feel as overwhelmed, and you can approach each task with more focus and intention.

Plus, breaking up the project can help you avoid the temptation to procrastinate. Sometimes, when we're faced with a big task, we put it off out of fear or anxiety. But if you break it up into smaller pieces, it's easier to get started and keep going.

So, the next time you're faced with a big project, try breaking it up into smaller tasks. Trust me, it'll make a huge difference!

Avoid distractions.

We all know how tempting it can be to take a break and scroll through social media or check our text messages, but sometimes that can lead to major distractions that can take us away from our work.

To avoid these kinds of distractions, try putting your phone on silent and closing any unnecessary tabs on your computer. You can also find a quiet space to work, like a coffee shop or a library, where you can stay focused and avoid the temptation to procrastinate.

Trust me, it's important to take breaks and recharge, but it's also important to stay focused and avoid distractions when it's time to get stuff done. So, next time you're working on a project, try minimizing distractions and see how much more productive you can be!

Prioritize rest.

It's easy to get caught up in work and forget to take a breather once in a while. But listen up, rest is just as important as work!

If you're feeling overwhelmed and burnt out, take a day off to recharge. Spend time doing things that make you happy and relaxed, like hanging out with friends, watching your favourite show, or taking a long nap. Trust me, taking time to recharge your batteries will help you be more productive and focused in the long run.

So, don't be afraid to take a day off every once in a while. Your brain and body will thank you for it! And when you return to work, you'll have renewed energy and motivation to tackle whatever projects come your way.

In conclusion, procrastination doesn't have to be a negative habit. By embracing "Zen procrastination," we can turn our natural inclination towards doing nothing into a productive habit. By taking intentional breaks, doing nothing on purpose, breaking up big tasks, avoiding distractions, and prioritizing rest, we can approach our work with a renewed sense of energy and focus. So, next time you feel the urge to procrastinate, embrace the pause and see how it can work for you.

Don't Let Your Desk Become a Black Hole: The Art of Organization

Have you ever looked at your desk and wondered how it became such a mess? Piles of paper, scattered office supplies, and a general feeling of disarray can make it hard to focus and be productive. But fear not - with a little organization, you can turn your desk into a functional workspace that fosters creativity and productivity.

The art of organization isn't just about cleaning up your physical space, it's about creating a system that works for you. Here are some tips for how to organize your desk and boost your productivity:

Start with a clean slate.

First things first, you got to get rid of all the clutter before you can even start organizing your desk. So, take everything off your desk and sort them into piles. Keep the stuff you use all the time within reach, and stash away anything that you don't need regularly in a drawer or filing cabinet. This will give you a blank canvas to work with and make it easier to get your space sorted out.

Once you've cleared your desk, it's time to start organizing. Look at the items on your desk and group them by category. For example, put all your pens and pencils together, stack your papers in one pile, and gather all your electronics in another. This will help you see what you have and make it easier to find what you need when you need it.

Next, invest in some storage solutions that work for you. This could be anything from file folders to desk trays to small containers for your loose items. Make sure everything has a designated place and try to keep like items together. This will not only make your desk look more organized but also help you work more efficiently.

Lastly, make it a habit to regularly declutter and tidy up your desk. Set aside a few minutes each day to put things away and keep your space organized. Trust me, you'll feel more productive and less stressed with a neat and tidy desk!

Create zones.

When organizing your desk, it's important to think about the different activities you perform at your desk and create designated areas for each task. This will help you keep your desk organized and make it easier to find what you need quickly. You can create zones based on the different tasks you do, like writing, filing, or office supplies.

To create zones, start by grouping together the items you use for each task. For example, gather all your pens, pencils, and markers for your writing zone. Then, consider the best location for each zone based on your workflow. You might want your writing zone to be near a window for natural light, while your filing zone may be better located near your file cabinet.

When you've created your zones, keep them clearly defined by using containers or trays to keep items within each zone. This will help prevent clutter from spreading and keep everything in its designated spot. By creating designated zones, you'll make it easier to find what you need, and you'll be less likely to let clutter build up over time.

Use storage solutions.

If you want to keep your desk organized, it's important to invest in storage solutions that work for you. This could mean anything from file folders to drawer organizers to desk trays. The key is to choose solutions that fit your specific needs and your personal style so that you're more likely to use them consistently.

When shopping for storage solutions, consider factors like size, durability, and accessibility. You want to choose products that are the right size for the items you need to store, that are sturdy enough to hold up over time, and that is easy to access so you don't have to struggle to find what you're looking for.

Another important consideration is the aesthetics of your storage solutions. If you're someone who cares about the appearance of your workspace, you may want to choose storage solutions that are stylish or that match your existing decor. On the other hand, if you're more focused on functionality than aesthetics, you might prioritize storage solutions that are practical and easy to use, even if they're not the most visually appealing.

Overall, investing in the right storage solutions can make a big difference in how organized and productive you are at work. By taking the time to find the products that work best for you, you can keep your desk clutter-free and make it easier to focus on the tasks at hand.

Keep it simple.

Keeping your desk organized doesn't have to be complicated. In fact, the key to success is to keep it simple. Rather than implementing multiple complex systems, focus on the essentials and find what works best for you. The simpler the system, the easier it will be to maintain your organized desk over time.

By keeping your desk organization simple and tailored to your specific needs, you'll create a space that's both functional and aesthetically pleasing.

Get rid of unnecessary items.

If there's something on your desk that you haven't used in ages, it's time to say goodbye. All that clutter can make it hard to focus on the things you actually need. Consider donating, recycling, or tossing things you no longer need or use. This can help clear out space for the things you actually use and make your desk feel less overwhelming.

Remember, less is more when it comes to desk organization. Only keep the things that are essential and help you do your job efficiently. If you're unsure about an item, ask yourself when was the last time you used it, and if you're likely to use it again in the future. If the answer is no, it's time to let go.

Keeping your desk organized doesn't have to be complicated, and a little bit of decluttering can go a long way. By keeping only what you need and use, you can create a clean and functional workspace that will help you be more productive and efficient.

Use labels.

Labels are a great way to keep your desk organized and save time when looking for things. Label file folders, storage containers, and any other items you use regularly to make them easier to locate. Labels can be created using a label maker or written by hand, whichever is more convenient for you. When you label items, make sure the labels are clear and easy to read. This will prevent any confusion or frustration when trying to find something in a hurry. If you need to change the contents of a container or folder, simply change the label so that it reflects the new contents. By using labels, you'll be able to quickly identify what you need and keep your desk looking neat and tidy.

Clean up at the end of the day.

After a long day at work, it's tempting to leave your desk as is and just head out the door. However, taking a few minutes to tidy up can make a big difference. It'll help you start the next day with a clean slate and reduce stress in the morning. Set aside five to ten minutes at the end of each day to put away supplies and materials, file papers, and straighten up your workspace.

If you're in a rush, prioritize putting away supplies and materials. These items can quickly add up and clutter your desk, making it difficult to find what you need the next day. Next, file any papers you don't need immediate access to. This will prevent them from piling up and becoming overwhelming. Finally, take a quick scan of your desk and straighten up anything that's out of place. This can be a quick and easy way to create a sense of order and calm in your workspace.

By taking a few minutes each day to clean up your desk, you'll create a positive habit that will benefit you in the long run. Plus, you'll feel more productive and accomplished at the end of each day.

In conclusion, the organization is key to creating a functional and productive workspace. By starting with a clean slate, creating zones, using storage solutions, keeping it simple, getting rid of unnecessary items, using labels, and cleaning up at the end of each day, you can turn your desk into a well-organized space that fosters creativity and productivity. Don't let your desk become a black hole - take control of your space and see how it can boost your productivity and overall well-being.

Why Your Co-workers Aren't Mind Readers: Effective Communication Strategies in the Workplace

Effective communication is essential in any workplace. When co-workers understand each other's expectations, it can lead to increased productivity, higher job satisfaction, and a more positive work environment. However, many people struggle with effective communication in the workplace, assuming that their co-workers will understand their needs or expectations without explicit communication. In reality, your co-workers aren't minded readers, and effective communication is necessary to ensure everyone is on the same page.

Here are some reasons why communication is important in the workplace:

Avoiding misunderstandings

Sometimes people assume others know what they're thinking or what needs to be done, but that's not always the case. It's important to speak up and communicate clearly to avoid misunderstandings. If someone doesn't explain something fully or assumes others know what they mean, it can lead to a lot of problems. Confusion, frustration, and even arguments can happen when people don't communicate effectively.

To prevent this from happening, it's crucial to be open and honest when communicating. If something is unclear, ask questions and seek clarification. Don't assume that others know what you're thinking or what needs to be done. By taking the time to communicate clearly, you can avoid misunderstandings and prevent unnecessary stress and tension in the workplace.

Building relationships

Good communication skills are essential for building strong relationships with your co-workers. When everyone communicates effectively, it creates a sense of trust and respect, which makes the workplace a happier and more positive environment. It's important to make sure you're being clear and concise when you're speaking to someone, and that you're actively listening to what they have to say in return. When everyone feels like they can share their thoughts and ideas freely, it can lead to more collaboration and innovation, which benefits everyone on the team.

So don't be afraid to speak up and ask questions, and always try to be mindful of how your words and actions are being received by others. A little effort towards good communication can go a long way towards building a better workplace culture.

Improving productivity

When co-workers know how to talk to each other effectively, work gets done faster and better. When everyone understands what they need to do, they can get it done in less time, which is awesome for the business. Plus, when the team is communicating well, it creates a more positive and productive work environment. It's way easier to work on tasks when you know that everyone is working towards the same goals and can support each other. Good communication can make all the difference in achieving success as a team.

Now that we know why communication is important in the workplace, here are some effective communication strategies to consider:

Be clear and concise.

When you're talking to your colleagues, try to keep it simple and straightforward. Don't use fancy words or technical terms that not everyone will understand. Stick to plain language and be concise. This will help to avoid confusion and misunderstandings, and make sure that everyone is on the same page. Plus, it can help to save time by not having to explain things over and over again. So, whether you're sending an email or having a conversation, think about your words carefully and choose them wisely. Your colleagues will appreciate it, and it'll help to build trust and respect in the workplace.

Listen actively.

When chatting with your co-workers, it's not just about speaking your mind - listening is just as important! When your colleague is speaking, actively engage with them and respond thoughtfully. It shows that you value their perspective and are committed to understanding their point of view. Good communication is a two-way street, and both talking and listening are important skills to master.

To listen effectively, try to give your co-worker your full attention. Avoid distractions and really focus on what they're saying. You might also try summarizing what they've said to make sure you understand correctly. And don't forget to respond appropriately - this could be as simple as nodding your head or offering a thoughtful response.

Remember, communication is a crucial part of any successful workplace, and effective listening is a key component. When everyone feels heard and valued, it can lead to better collaboration and a more positive work environment overall.

Be respectful.

When it comes to talking to your co-workers, showing them respect is super important. It's all about treating them how you'd like to be treated. If you value their input, they'll value yours too. Respectful communication can help create a positive work environment where people feel comfortable sharing their thoughts and ideas.

Listening to your co-workers is also essential to show respect for them. When they're speaking, try to give them your full attention and respond appropriately. By actively listening, you're showing that you value their opinion and are invested in the conversation. This can also help avoid misunderstandings and make sure everyone is on the same page.

Use the right communication method.

When it comes to communicating with your co-workers, it's important to choose the right method for the situation. Sending an email may be great for sharing information quickly, but it may not be the best way to discuss a complex issue. In those cases, a face-to-face meeting may be more appropriate. By choosing the right communication method, you can ensure that your message is received in the best possible way.

For instance, if you need to discuss a sensitive matter with a co-worker, it may be better to talk in person rather than sending an email. This will allow you to read their body language and tone of voice, which can help you better understand their perspective. On the other hand, if you're just sharing an update on a project, an email may be more efficient than scheduling a meeting.

The key is to consider the situation and the message you're trying to convey, and then choose the best communication method for that scenario. This will help ensure that your message is received effectively and that you're able to communicate with your co-workers in the most efficient and productive way possible.

Give feedback.

It's important to give feedback regularly. This helps everyone understand what's expected of them and make improvements where necessary. Whether it's positive feedback or constructive criticism, it's essential for effective communication.

Remember, feedback should be specific and focused on behaviours or actions, rather than personal attacks. It's also important to make sure you're giving feedback in a timely manner, rather than waiting until a problem has escalated.

Giving and receiving feedback can be a little uncomfortable at first, but it's an important part of communication and can lead to growth and improvement for everyone involved. So don't be afraid to speak up and share your thoughts with your co-workers!

Use nonverbal cues.

Your body language and tone of voice can also communicate a lot to your co-workers. So, it's important to pay attention to these nonverbal cues to make sure you're communicating effectively. It's not just what you say that matters, but how you say it.

For instance, if you're speaking with someone and you're slouching in your chair, looking away or frowning, it could convey that you're not interested or don't care about what they're saying. Similarly, if you speak in a monotone or aggressive tone, it can make the other person feel uncomfortable or defensive.

On the other hand, positive nonverbal cues like smiling, making eye contact, nodding, or leaning forward can show that you're engaged and interested in the conversation. This can help build rapport and make it easier for others to open up and communicate with you.

So, always try to be aware of your nonverbal cues and use them appropriately to help convey your message effectively.

Follow up.

It's crucial to follow up with your co-workers after having a conversation or meeting. It helps everyone to be on the same page and avoid any confusion. Sending a quick email or message to recap the discussion can ensure that everyone understands the next steps and responsibilities. It also helps to clarify any misunderstandings that may have occurred during the conversation. Following up can save you and your team time and prevent mistakes from happening.

Moreover, following up is a way to show that you're accountable and responsible. It demonstrates that you value your co-workers' time and input, and that you take the discussion seriously. Following up can also help to build trust and foster positive working relationships. When people feel heard and acknowledged, they're more likely to be invested in the success of the project or task at hand. So, don't forget to follow up and make sure everyone is on the same page!

In conclusion, effective communication is key to a positive work environment and increased productivity. By being clear and concise, listening actively, being respectful, using the right communication method, giving feedback, using nonverbal cues, and following up, you can communicate more effectively with your co-workers. Remember, your co-workers aren't mind readers, so it's important to communicate openly and clearly to avoid misunderstandings and build positive relationships in the workplace.

How to Survive a Meeting Without Falling Asleep: The Ultimate Guide to Staying Awake

Meetings are an essential part of business communication. They can help to coordinate and plan work, share information, and make important decisions. However, meetings can also be tedious and unproductive, leading to boredom and even falling asleep. If you struggle with staying awake in meetings, don't worry - you're not alone. Here are some tips to help you stay awake and engaged during meetings:

Prepare yourself.

To ensure you're fully prepared for a meeting, it's important to take care of your physical well-being beforehand. This means getting enough rest the night before, so you're well-rested and alert. It's also important to fuel your body with a healthy breakfast and stay hydrated by drinking plenty of water. This will help keep your energy levels up and your mind sharp.

If you're feeling drowsy or sluggish, it's a good idea to take a quick break and do some stretching or light exercise. This will get your blood flowing and help wake you up. Even just a short walk around the block can do wonders for your alertness and concentration.

It's also helpful to arrive at the meeting a few minutes early, so you can gather your thoughts and mentally prepare yourself for the discussion ahead. Take a few deep breaths and focus on your intentions for the meeting. This can help you stay centred and engaged throughout the discussion.

By taking care of your physical and mental well-being before a meeting, you can ensure that you're fully present and able to contribute meaningfully to the discussion.

Get involved.

To avoid zoning out during a meeting, it's important to actively participate. Engaging in the discussion by asking questions, sharing your thoughts, and offering solutions is a great way to stay focused and prevent your mind from wandering. Active participation can also help you gain a better understanding of the topic at hand and contribute to a more productive meeting.

Additionally, it's helpful to avoid distractions during the meeting. Close any unnecessary tabs or apps on your computer or phone to prevent notifications from disrupting your focus. Try to keep eye contact with the speaker and avoid looking at other things on your screen or in the room.

Overall, active participation and minimizing distractions are key to staying engaged in a meeting and making the most out of the discussion.

Take notes.

If you find yourself struggling to stay engaged in a meeting, taking notes could be a good way to help you stay focused. Not only does it give you something to do with your hands, but it also helps you retain important information. When taking notes, try to be as detailed as possible, but don't stress too much about getting everything down word for word. The most important thing is to keep yourself engaged and alert.

To make notetaking even more effective, consider using different techniques, such as mind mapping or bullet points. Mind mapping can be a great way to connect ideas and visualize relationships between different topics discussed in the meeting. Bullet points are a more traditional method that can help you organize information in a clear and concise way.

When taking notes, try to focus on the key points of the discussion and any action items that need to be addressed. This will help you stay on track and ensure that you are actively participating in the meeting. By taking notes, you can also refer back to the discussion later on, which can be helpful when following up on action items or trying to recall important information.

Drink caffeine

Coffee, tea, or a caffeinated soda can provide a quick energy boost to help you stay awake and focused. However, it's important to remember that too much caffeine can make you feel jittery and anxious, so it's best not to overdo it.

If you're going to rely on caffeine to keep you going, it's important to plan ahead. Make sure you have a cup of coffee or tea before the meeting starts so that the caffeine has time to take effect. Additionally, be mindful of the caffeine content in your drinks – some beverages, like energy drinks, can contain a lot of caffeine and may not be the best choice if you're sensitive to it.

While caffeine can be a helpful tool, it's not a substitute for a good night's sleep and proper hydration. If you find yourself relying on caffeine too often, it might be a sign that you need to make some changes to your sleep habits or find other ways to stay alert and focused during meetings.

Avoid sugar.

If you're feeling tired during a meeting, it might be tempting to reach for a sugary snack or drink to get a quick energy boost. However, this might not be the best strategy. Sugar can give you a brief rush of energy, but it can also lead to a crash that leaves you feeling even more tired than before. Instead, try to choose healthy snacks like fruit, nuts, or vegetables, and make sure to stay hydrated by drinking plenty of water.

Fruits like apples, bananas, and berries are good options because they contain natural sugars that can give you a boost of energy without the crash. Nuts like almonds or walnuts can also be a good choice as they provide healthy fats and protein that can keep you feeling full and focused. Vegetables like carrots or celery can also provide a satisfying crunch that can help keep you alert during the meeting.

In addition to healthy snacks, make sure to stay hydrated by drinking plenty of water. Dehydration can cause fatigue, so it's important to keep water on hand and take sips throughout the meeting. By choosing healthy snacks and staying hydrated, you'll be better equipped to stay alert and engaged during the meeting.

Change positions.

If you're having trouble staying awake during a meeting, changing your physical position can be a helpful trick to stay alert. Adjusting your posture by sitting up straight, crossing your legs, or leaning forward can help you maintain focus and avoid dozing off. Moving around or standing up if possible can also help you stay engaged and awake.

When you sit in the same position for an extended period, your body can become numb or stiff, causing you to feel tired and lethargic. Changing your position can increase blood flow to different parts of your body and help you feel more awake and alert.

If you're in a virtual meeting and cannot move around as much, you can also try adjusting your screen's position, increasing the font size, or changing the lighting to help you stay focused.

Remember, staying engaged in a meeting requires a combination of physical and mental strategies. Don't hesitate to speak up, take notes, or ask questions to keep your mind active and alert.

Focus on the speaker.

Meetings can be long and often filled with information that may not be very interesting. It's essential to focus on the speaker and actively listen to what they're saying to stay engaged. If you're finding it hard to stay focused, try to look for something interesting in what they're saying or find connections between what they're saying and your own work. This will help you stay engaged and keep your mind from wandering.

Additionally, if there are distractions in the room, try to eliminate them. Turn off your phone or put it on silent mode, close unnecessary tabs on your computer, and minimize any other potential distractions. It's also important to take breaks when needed. Excuse yourself for a few minutes and take a quick walk or stretch your legs. This will help you to clear your mind and come back to the meeting with renewed focus.

Finally, it's essential to stay positive and motivated. Remind yourself of the meeting's purpose and what you hope to gain from it. If you're having trouble staying positive, try to think of some potential benefits or outcomes that could come from the meeting. This will help you stay engaged and focused on the task at hand.

Take breaks.

Sitting through a long and boring meeting can be a real challenge, but taking breaks can make it more bearable. If you find yourself struggling to concentrate or feeling restless, try to take a break when you can. Excuse yourself to go to the restroom or grab a drink of water to stretch your legs and get a change of scenery. This will help you to stay refreshed and re-energized, making it easier to stay focused on the meeting.

If you're unable to leave the meeting, try to find ways to take a break without being too obvious. For example, you could try stretching your legs under the table or discreetly checking your phone. Just be sure not to disrupt the meeting or draw too much attention to yourself.

Another way to break up a long meeting is to engage with the speaker or other participants. Ask questions or offer your opinion to keep your mind active and engaged. This can also help to make the meeting more productive by encouraging others to participate and contribute their ideas.

Overall, taking breaks and finding ways to stay engaged can help make a long and tedious meeting more bearable. Remember to take care of yourself and try not to get too overwhelmed by the length of the meeting.

In conclusion, staying awake during meetings can be a challenge, but it's essential for effective communication and productivity. By preparing yourself beforehand, actively participating, taking notes, drinking caffeine in moderation, avoiding sugar, changing positions, focusing on the speaker, and taking breaks when you can, you can stay engaged and alert throughout the meeting. Remember, falling asleep in a meeting is not only unprofessional, but it can also lead to missed opportunities and ineffective communication. Use these tips to stay awake and make the most of your next meeting.

Why Multi-Tasking is Overrated: The Art of Single-Tasking for Increased Productivity"

In today's fast-paced world, multi-tasking is often seen as a badge of honour. We're told that we need to be able to juggle multiple tasks at once in order to be productive and successful. But the truth is that multi-tasking can actually be detrimental to productivity and lead to burnout. In this article, we'll explore the art of single-tasking and why it's a more effective way to increase productivity.

What is single-tasking?

Basically, it means doing one thing at a time without any interruptions. When you focus on a single task, you're able to give it your full attention and do it more efficiently. This can lead to better results because you're not trying to do a million things at once and getting overwhelmed.

Imagine you're trying to write an important email while also checking your social media and responding to text messages. It's hard to focus on what you're writing when you're constantly switching between tasks. Single-tasking means closing your social media and putting your phone on silent so you can give your email your full attention.

So, if you want to work more effectively, try single-tasking. It might take some practice, but you'll soon realize that you can accomplish more by focusing on one task at a time.

Why is multi-tasking overrated?

You might think that doing two or more things at once is the way to get more done in less time, but it's actually a big fat lie. Studies have shown that multi-tasking can do more harm than good. Why, you ask? Well, our brains aren't wired to handle several tasks simultaneously. When we try to do too much at once, our focus and attention get scattered, leading to mistakes, missed opportunities, and an overall decrease in productivity.

Multi-tasking can also be a recipe for burnout. Constantly juggling a bunch of tasks can be stressful and exhausting, which can take a toll on our mental and physical health. This can lead to a lack of motivation, decreased productivity, and an overall drop in job satisfaction. It's like being on a hamster wheel that never stops, and that's no way to live.

So, what's the solution? It's simple - single-tasking. Single-tasking is all about focusing on one thing at a time without distractions or interruptions. It's about being present in the moment and giving your full attention to the task at hand. When you're fully focused on one thing, you're able to work more efficiently and effectively, which can lead to better results.

Now, I know it's not always easy to single-task. We live in a world full of distractions, from social media notifications to emails pinging in our inbox. But the key is to create an environment that's conducive to single-tasking. That might mean turning off your phone notifications, closing your email tab, or finding a quiet space to work. You could also try breaking your work down into smaller, more manageable tasks, and focus on completing them one by one.

At the end of the day, single-tasking is a mindset. It's about valuing the task at hand and giving it the attention it deserves. So, if you're feeling overwhelmed and unproductive, give single-tasking a try. You might just be surprised by how much you can accomplish when you're fully focused on one thing.

How does single-tasking improve productivity?

Single-tasking is pretty cool. It's all about concentrating on one thing at a time without being interrupted or distracted. When we do that, we're more likely to do a great job and achieve better results. Plus, we can say bye-bye to those pesky interruptions that always seem to pop up and get in the way of getting things done.

Another awesome thing about single-tasking is that it can help us avoid burnout. When we try to do too many things at once, it can be stressful and exhausting. But when we focus on one thing at a time, we can reduce stress and improve our job satisfaction. We'll feel a sense of accomplishment when we finish a task, which can give us a boost of motivation and help us enjoy our work more.

So if you want to be more efficient, effective, and stress-free, try single-tasking! Give it a shot and see how it works for you.

Tips for implementing single-tasking:

1. *Prioritize your tasks:* Start by identifying the most important tasks you need to complete each day. Prioritize these tasks and focus on them one at a time, rather than trying to do everything at once.

2. *Eliminate distractions:* Turn off your phone notifications, close your email inbox, and shut your office door if possible. This will help you to eliminate distractions and stay focused on the task at hand.

3. *Take breaks:* While it's important to focus on one task at a time, it's also important to take breaks throughout the day. Taking short breaks can help to improve focus and productivity, and can help to prevent burnout.

4. *Use a timer:* Set a timer for a specific amount of time, such as 25 or 30 minutes, and focus solely on the task at hand during that time. This technique, known as the Pomodoro Technique, can help you to stay focused and avoid distractions.

5. *Practice mindfulness*: Mindfulness is the practice of being fully present in the moment. When you're working on a task, try to be fully present and focus on the task at hand, rather than letting your mind wander.

In conclusion, multi-tasking may be overrated when it comes to productivity. Instead, focusing on single-tasking can help to improve focus, reduce stress, and increase job satisfaction. By prioritizing tasks, eliminating distractions, taking breaks, using a timer, and practicing mindfulness, you can implement single-tasking techniques and achieve better results in your work and personal life.

Dealing With Difficult Co-workers: A Survival Guide

In every workplace, there are bound to be difficult co-workers. These are the people who seem to thrive on drama, who always have something negative to say, and who can make your work life miserable. Dealing with difficult co-workers can be challenging, but it's not impossible. In this article, we'll provide you with a survival guide for dealing with difficult co-workers and maintaining your sanity in the workplace.

Stay Calm

When it comes to dealing with difficult co-workers, keeping your cool is key. You don't want to get all worked up and let your emotions get the better of you. That's only going to make things worse! Instead, take a step back, take a deep breath, and try to assess the situation calmly. Don't be too quick to react or say something you might regret later on. It's better to take a little time to think things through and come up with a more measured response. This will help you to keep the situation from escalating and may even help to diffuse tensions between you and your co-worker.

Don't Take it Personally.

Dealing with tough co-workers can be a real headache, but it's important not to let their bad vibes get to you. Remember, they're probably just lashing out because of their own problems, and it's not about you personally. So, try not to take it too personally, and instead, focus on the facts of the situation.

Take a step back, breathe deep, and think about what's really going on. Are they upset about a specific project or task? Is there something going on in their personal life that's causing them stress? Try to put yourself in their shoes and see things from their perspective. This can help you to find a solution that works for both of you.

Remember, it's okay to set boundaries and stand up for yourself if their behaviour is crossing a line. But it's important to do so in a calm and professional manner. Don't react impulsively or say something that you might regret later. Instead, focus on finding a solution that works for everyone involved.

Set Boundaries

Dealing with co-workers who can't respect your boundaries can be a real pain in the butt. But don't worry, you've got this! The key is to be clear and direct about what you're willing to put up with and what you're not. If someone's trying to dump extra work on you or drag you into a negative conversation, don't be afraid to say "no." Stand your ground and let them know that you won't tolerate that kind of behaviour.

But here's the thing: you don't have to be a jerk about it. It's possible to be assertive without being aggressive. Be polite and professional, but firm. Remember, you have a right to your boundaries, and it's up to you to enforce them. So if your co-worker is pushing your buttons, take a deep breath, and calmly but firmly let them know that you won't be walked all over. You'll be surprised at how much better you feel when you stand up for yourself!

Communicate Effectively

When it comes to dealing with difficult co-workers, communication is crucial. And by communication, we don't mean just talking, but also listening actively. It's important to keep your cool and not let their behaviour get to you, even if they're being a pain in the butt. And one way to do that is by using "I" statements instead of "you" statements. Saying "I feel frustrated when..." is much better than "You always do this...". It's less accusatory and more about how their actions affect you.

But communication is a two-way street, so make sure to also listen to what they have to say. Sometimes, difficult co-workers just need to vent or feel heard. Show them that you're willing to listen and find a solution that works for both of you. And if you're not sure what they want or need, don't be afraid to ask. Clear communication can help to prevent misunderstandings and conflicts in the future.

Seek Support

Dealing with difficult co-workers can be a real pain in the butt, and it can take a toll on your mental health. That's why it's important to get support from others when you're dealing with these kinds of situations. You don't have to go it alone! Try talking to someone you trust, like a co-worker, your supervisor, or even a friend outside of work. Share what's been going on and how you're feeling. Sometimes just getting things off your chest can help you feel better and gain some perspective on the situation. If things are really bad, you might even want to consider talking to a professional counsellor. There's no shame in seeking help when you need it, and a counsellor can help you develop coping strategies and give you the tools you need to deal with difficult people in a healthy way. So don't suffer in silence - reach out for help!

Document Everything

When you've got a difficult co-worker who's acting out of line, it's essential to keep a paper trail of everything that's happening. Jot down the date, time, and a brief description of any incidents that occur, no matter how small they might seem at the time. This will help you build a solid case if you need to bring the issue to your supervisor or HR department.

Make sure to document the behaviour as objectively as possible, without getting emotional or personal. Stick to the facts and avoid any assumptions or interpretations. Having a clear record of what happened and when will help you to explain the situation to others and demonstrate that you've tried to resolve the issue on your own.

Remember, though, that documentation should be a last resort. Try to resolve the situation through communication and other means before resorting to documenting everything. But if the situation escalates or continues to be a problem, having a record of what's been going on can be invaluable.

Know When to Escalate

When you've had it up to here with a difficult co-worker and you've exhausted all other options, it's time to take things to the next level. That means going to your boss or HR and spilling the tea about what's been going on. Don't hold back, tell them everything that's been happening and how it's affecting your work and wellbeing. They may be able to offer some support, or even mediate a discussion between you and your difficult colleague.

If the situation is really extreme, you might need to bring in some outside help. This could be a lawyer or a union rep, someone who can advocate for your rights and help you navigate the legal or contractual issues involved. Whatever you do, don't suffer in silence. You deserve to work in an environment that is safe and respectful, and sometimes that means standing up for yourself and taking action.

In conclusion, dealing with difficult co-workers can be challenging, but it's not impossible. By staying calm, not taking it personally, setting boundaries, communicating effectively, seeking support, documenting everything, and knowing when to escalate, you can effectively deal with difficult co-workers and maintain your sanity in the workplace. Remember that you have the power to control how you respond to difficult co-workers and that by remaining professional and respectful, you can create a positive work environment for yourself and those around you.

Why You Should Embrace Feedback (Even When It Hurts): The Importance of Constructive Criticism

Feedback is a critical component of personal and professional growth. It provides us with an opportunity to learn and improve by giving us insight into how others perceive our actions, behaviours, and performance. However, feedback can also be challenging, especially when it's negative or critical. In this article, we'll discuss why you should embrace feedback, even when it hurts, and the importance of constructive criticism in personal and professional development.

Feedback Helps You Grow

Feedback can be a real game-changer when it comes to your personal and professional growth. Getting feedback from others can give you a fresh perspective on your actions, behaviours, and how you're performing. This new insight can be super helpful in pinpointing areas where you can improve and up your game. If you don't get any feedback, it can be tough to know where you stand and what you need to work on. That's why feedback is so crucial in identifying areas for growth and development. So, don't be afraid to ask for feedback, and be open to hearing what others have to say. It might just help you reach your full potential!

Feedback Increases Self-Awareness

Getting feedback from others is crucial to becoming more self-aware. When you get feedback, it forces you to take a step back and think about how others see you. This can help you to recognize your strengths and weaknesses and give you the opportunity to improve. Without feedback, it's easy to become complacent and miss out on opportunities for personal and professional growth.

Being self-aware is key to success in all areas of life, whether it's in the workplace or in personal relationships. It can help you to identify your own biases, recognize your own limitations, and understand how your actions impact others. Plus, the more self-aware you are, the better you can communicate with others and build stronger relationships.

So don't be afraid to ask for feedback or accept it when it's offered. Even if it's not always easy to hear, it can help you become a better version of yourself in the long run.

Feedback Helps You Improve Relationships

Feedback is something important when it comes to building and keeping good relationships. When someone gives you feedback, it means they give a damn about your success and want to see you do well. Being open to feedback shows that you respect and value other people's opinions and that you're committed to making things better in your relationships. So, don't be shy about asking for feedback or taking it in. It can help you learn more about how to work with others, what you're doing right, and what you could do better. Plus, it can lead to more trust and respect between you and the people you work with. So, next time someone gives you feedback, don't get defensive, just take it in stride and use it as a way to grow and improve.

Feedback Helps You Avoid Blind Spots

Sometimes we don't see things the way others do, and that's where feedback comes in. It can help us spot our blind spots, or those areas where we're not aware of how our actions or behaviours affect others. By getting feedback, we can uncover these blind spots and work on addressing them. This can be super important, as ignoring blind spots can lead to all kinds of problems, like missed opportunities, damaged relationships, and lower performance. Being open to feedback and willing to listen can help you catch these blind spots before they become major issues. So don't be afraid to ask for feedback or accept it when it's given, even if it's not easy to hear. It could make all the difference in your personal and professional life.

Feedback Increases Accountability

When someone gives you feedback, it's like they're giving you a little nudge to take responsibility for your actions and improve your game. Being open to feedback shows that you're willing to own up to your mistakes and do what it takes to get better. This level of accountability can really make a difference in how people perceive you and your abilities, both in your personal life and on the job. So, next time someone gives you feedback, don't brush it off or get defensive. Take it on the chin and use it to make positive changes in your behaviour. You'll be surprised at the difference it can make.

Feedback Helps You Develop Resilience

Getting feedback, especially when it's not all sunshine and rainbows, can be tough. But here's the deal, if you can learn to accept and even appreciate feedback, you'll build up your resilience. This means you'll be better equipped to handle the tough times, recover quicker, and come back even stronger.

Feedback helps you to learn from your mistakes, grow and become a better version of yourself. Even if the feedback feels like a punch to the gut, take a deep breath and see if there's something valuable you can take away from it. By doing this, you'll be able to turn negative feedback into an opportunity for growth and development.

Remember, feedback isn't always easy to hear, but it can be a valuable tool for building resilience and improving yourself. So, be open to feedback, keep an open mind, and keep pushing forward. You got this!

Feedback Helps You Achieve Your Goals

Getting feedback is crucial to achieving your goals, plain and simple. When you're open to feedback, you can identify areas where you need to improve and work on developing the skills and behaviours necessary to reach your goals. Without feedback, it's like driving without a map – you might eventually get where you want to go, but you're more likely to take a wrong turn or miss an important landmark. Feedback helps keep you on track and makes sure you don't miss any key opportunities for growth and development. So, don't be afraid to ask for feedback or to receive it, even if it's not all sunshine and rainbows. It's all part of the journey towards reaching your goals, and in the end, it'll be worth it.

In conclusion, feedback is essential in personal and professional growth and development. By embracing feedback, even when it hurts, you can improve your self-awareness, build positive relationships, avoid blind spots, increase accountability, develop resilience, and achieve your goals. Remember that feedback, even when it's negative, is not a reflection of your worth as a person. Instead, it's an opportunity to learn, grow, and become the best version of yourself.

Why You Should Never Hit 'Reply All': Email Etiquette in the Workplace

Email is a critical tool for communication in the workplace. It allows us to share information, collaborate with colleagues, and stay organized. However, email can also be a source of frustration and confusion, especially when people don't follow proper email etiquette. One of the most significant email etiquette rules is to never hit "reply all" unless it's absolutely necessary. In this article, we'll discuss why hitting "reply all" can be problematic and the importance of email etiquette in the workplace.

It Can Lead to Information Overload

Hitting "reply all" can be a real pain in the butt because it can lead to an overload of information. When you hit "reply all," every single person on the email chain gets your response, whether they need to see it or not. This can cause a lot of unnecessary emails to flood everyone's inboxes, making it tough to find the important information buried in there. It's like throwing a bunch of junk mail in your mailbox - you have to sift through it all just to find the one piece of mail you actually need. So, it's a good idea to think twice before hitting "reply all" and consider whether everyone really needs to see your response.

It Can Be Annoying to Others

When you hit "reply all," it can be super annoying to others. Only a few people might actually care about your response, but everyone on the email chain will get it. This means that people have to dig through a bunch of emails that don't matter to find the ones that do. It's like trying to find a needle in a haystack. If people start getting bombarded with irrelevant emails, they might start to ignore them altogether. This can cause a breakdown in communication, which is never a good thing. So, hitting "reply all" can not only be frustrating, but it can also lead to important messages being missed. It's best to only use "reply all" when it's necessary and relevant to everyone on the email chain. Otherwise, it's best to just respond directly to the people who need to know.

It Can Create Confusion

When you hit "reply all" in response to a particular comment or question in an email chain, it can create confusion for other people trying to follow the conversation. It becomes challenging to keep track of who said what and in what order. This can lead to misunderstandings and mistakes that are time-consuming to correct. For example, if you respond to a question that was already answered earlier in the email chain, people may think that the answer is different or incomplete. This can create confusion, and people may start to question the accuracy of the information being shared. Additionally, when people start responding to the same email thread with multiple "reply all" responses, it becomes hard to track the relevant information. The result is often a breakdown in communication, which can lead to missed deadlines, misunderstandings, and mistakes. Therefore, it's essential to avoid hitting "reply all" unless it's absolutely necessary and relevant to all recipients.

It Can Be Unprofessional

When you hit "reply all" without considering if everyone needs to see your response, it can come across as unprofessional. This can create a negative impression of you, making you appear as if you're not taking the time to think about who needs to see your message. Your colleagues or clients may view this as careless or lazy, indicating a lack of professionalism and poor communication skills.

By being mindful of who needs to be included in the email chain, you can avoid the negative effects of hitting "reply all." This demonstrates that you're taking the time to consider who really needs to see your response and that you're a thoughtful and efficient communicator. Additionally, this helps to create a positive image of you in the minds of your colleagues and clients, which can be valuable in building trust and fostering good working relationships.

It Can Be Embarrassing

When you hit "reply all," you run the risk of sharing sensitive or confidential information with people who shouldn't have access to it. This can be incredibly embarrassing, damaging your reputation and relationships with colleagues. Even if you didn't share anything sensitive, hitting "reply all" can still be a source of embarrassment if you make a mistake or say something inappropriate.

In some cases, hitting "reply all" can even lead to disciplinary action. If you violate company policies or breach confidentiality by hitting "reply all," your actions can have serious consequences. This is especially true if the information you shared is related to sensitive topics such as HR or legal matters.

By being more mindful about when you hit "reply all," you can avoid these potential pitfalls. Taking the extra time to consider who really needs to see your response can save you a lot of headaches in the long run. It's always better to err on the side of caution and limit your response to only those who really need to see it.

So, what should you do instead of hitting "reply all"? If you want to avoid hitting "reply all" and causing a headache for everyone, here are some helpful tips to keep in mind:

1. *Think before you hit send.* Before you hit "reply all," ask yourself if your response is really necessary for everyone to see. If it's only relevant to a few people, consider sending a separate email instead.

2. *Use "reply" instead.* If you want to respond to an individual in the email chain, use the "reply" function instead of "reply all." This way, you can keep the conversation focused and avoid cluttering up inboxes.

3. *Be clear and concise.* When you do send an email, make sure your message is clear and to the point. Avoid unnecessary details or rambling, which can make it harder for people to understand what you're trying to say.

4. *Be mindful of tone.* Keep in mind that emails can be easily misinterpreted, so be mindful of your tone and how your message might come across. Use polite and professional language and avoid sarcasm or humour that might not translate well over email.

5. *Check your attachments.* Before you hit send, double-check to make sure you've attached any necessary files or documents. Forgetting an attachment can be frustrating for both you and the recipient, and can lead to unnecessary back-and-forth emails.

In conclusion, hitting "reply all" should be avoided unless it's absolutely necessary. By following proper email etiquette, you can reduce information overload, avoid annoying others, prevent confusion, maintain professionalism, and avoid embarrassment. Remember to think before you hit "reply all," be clear and concise, use proper salutations and signatures, and be mindful of your tone. By following these simple rules, you can communicate effectively and efficiently with your colleagues, while avoiding unnecessary email headaches.

The Power of Positive Thinking (And Positive People): How Your Attitude Affects Your Work

The importance of attitude in the workplace cannot be overstated. The way you approach your work can affect not only your own productivity but also that of your colleagues and the overall success of your organization. A positive attitude can make all the difference, and it's essential to understand the power of positive thinking.

Positive thinking is not just a buzzword or a feel-good sentiment. Research has shown that a positive attitude can have significant benefits for both your mental and physical health, as well as your work performance. By focusing on the positive aspects of your job and looking for solutions instead of dwelling on problems, you can increase your creativity, resilience, and ability to handle stress.

However, maintaining a positive attitude can be challenging, especially when faced with difficult situations or negative colleagues. That's why it's crucial to surround yourself with positive people who can offer support, encouragement, and constructive feedback. By building a network of positive relationships, you can create a more optimistic work environment and improve your chances of success.

Positive thinking is a mindset that focuses on the good things in life, rather than the negative. When you adopt a positive attitude, you're more likely to see opportunities rather than obstacles. You're more likely to take risks, try new things, and push yourself out of your comfort zone. Positive thinking can also help you cope with stress, overcome challenges, and stay motivated during difficult times.

One of the keys to positive thinking is to focus on your strengths rather than your weaknesses. When you focus on what you're good at, you'll feel more confident and capable, which can help you achieve your goals. You should also try to reframe negative thoughts into positive ones. For example, instead of thinking "I can't do this," try thinking "I can do this, I just need to figure out how."

Your attitude can have a significant impact on your work. If you have a positive attitude, you're more likely to be productive, creative, and successful. You'll be more willing to take on new challenges and collaborate with others. On the other hand, if you have a negative attitude, you're more likely to be unproductive, unmotivated, and unsuccessful. You'll be less willing to take risks and more likely to give up when things get difficult.

It's important to note that your attitude can also affect the attitudes of those around you. If you have a positive attitude, you're more likely to inspire and motivate your colleagues. Your positivity can be contagious, and can create a more supportive and productive work environment. On the other hand, if you have a negative attitude, you're more likely to bring others down and create a toxic work environment.

In addition to adopting a positive attitude yourself, it's important to surround yourself with positive people. Positive people can help you stay motivated and focused on your goals. They can also provide you with valuable support and encouragement when you need it most. Surrounding yourself with positive people can also help you maintain a positive attitude, even when things get difficult.

If you're looking to surround yourself with positive people, start by seeking out those who share your values and interests. Attend networking events, join a professional organization, or volunteer for a cause you're passionate about. You should also try to build relationships with colleagues who are positive and supportive. Seek out those who have a can-do attitude and are willing to help others succeed.

In conclusion, it is important to recognize that your attitude plays a crucial role in your work and overall success. A positive attitude can lead to improved performance, increased motivation, and better relationships with colleagues. By focusing on your strengths and surrounding yourself with positive people, you can create a supportive and encouraging work environment that can help you achieve your goals.

Furthermore, as you cultivate a positive attitude, remember that positivity is contagious. Your attitude can influence those around you, so make a conscious effort to spread positivity to your colleagues and team members. By doing so, you can create a ripple effect that will benefit everyone in the workplace.

In addition, don't forget the power of self-reflection and continuous improvement. Take the time to assess your attitudes and behaviours regularly, and make adjustments where necessary. This will help you maintain a positive outlook even in challenging situations, and help you to grow both personally and professionally.

Finally, always remember that a positive attitude is a choice. It may not always be easy, but by making a conscious effort to stay optimistic, you can create a more fulfilling and successful work life. So embrace positivity, focus on your strengths, and surround yourself with positive people – and watch as your career and life flourish.

Remember, positivity is contagious – so spread it around!

Why You Shouldn't Be a Lone Wolf: The Importance of Teamwork in the Workplace

In the modern-day, work culture has become fiercely competitive, with everyone striving to achieve individual goals and prove their worth. However, this cut-throat mentality often leads to people disregarding the value of working as a team. The idea of being a 'lone wolf' and working independently might seem appealing to some, but in reality, it can hinder personal and organizational growth.

The concept of teamwork is not new, yet it is often overlooked. The importance of teamwork in the workplace cannot be overstated. In today's fast-paced and complex work environment, where interdependence is inevitable, collaboration is key. The success of an organization depends on the collective efforts of its members working towards a common goal. It's only through teamwork that people can capitalize on their strengths, make up for their weaknesses, and achieve success.

Working as a team has many benefits. One of the most significant advantages is that it enables the sharing of ideas and knowledge. When people from diverse backgrounds and with different skills come together, they can bring a variety of ideas to the table. This promotes creativity and innovation, leading to more effective problem-solving and decision-making. A team also provides a forum for constructive feedback, which helps to improve the quality of work and enhances individual skills.

Moreover, working as a team instills a sense of ownership and responsibility. When people work together, they share both the successes and failures of the group. This creates a sense of accountability that motivates each team member to work towards their best potential. It also fosters a feeling of camaraderie and mutual support, which can boost morale and improve job satisfaction.

In contrast, working alone can be isolating and overwhelming. It's easy to feel stuck and unsure of how to proceed when one is working in isolation. The sense of responsibility for the entire workload can be daunting and stressful, leading to burnout and decreased productivity. When people work in teams, they can divide the workload and share the burden. This makes it easier to accomplish tasks and reduces the likelihood of feeling overwhelmed.

Teamwork is an essential component of success in the workplace. The ability to work well with others and harness the collective strength of a team is a valuable skill that should not be underestimated. The benefits of teamwork go beyond just achieving goals; it fosters a supportive and collaborative work culture that can lead to increased job satisfaction and overall success. Therefore, it is important to recognize the value of teamwork and to work towards building a strong team in any workplace.

But the benefits of teamwork go beyond simply getting things done. Working collaboratively also helps people build relationships and develop new skills. When people work together, they learn from each other and can take on new challenges that they might not have been able to tackle alone. Additionally, working in a team can be motivating and energizing, as people draw inspiration and support from each other.

Of course, working in a team is not always easy. It requires strong communication skills, the ability to manage conflict, and a willingness to compromise and be flexible. But these skills are essential in today's workplace, where teamwork and collaboration are increasingly becoming the norm. And even if you prefer to work independently, there will inevitably be times when you need to work with others in order to achieve your goals.

In conclusion, the importance of teamwork in the workplace cannot be overstated. Whether you consider yourself a natural collaborator or a self-proclaimed "lone wolf," the strategies and tips provided in this book can help you succeed in your professional life. By learning to embrace the power of teamwork, you can achieve your goals more effectively and efficiently than ever before. Remember that no one succeeds alone, and that by working collaboratively, you can accomplish great things. So, take the first step today, and start building your skills and relationships as a team player. With practice and determination, you'll soon find that the rewards of teamwork are well worth the effort.

How to Deal With an Overbearing Boss: A Guide to Navigating Difficult Relationships

Working under an overbearing boss can be a daunting experience, and it is easy to feel overwhelmed and demotivated in such a work environment. However, it is essential to realize that your boss's behaviour is not a reflection of your worth as an employee. Instead of giving up or suffering in silence, it is important to develop strategies to navigate difficult relationships with overbearing bosses. In fact, such challenges can provide an opportunity for you to grow and become a stronger, more resilient employee.

While it may seem easier to avoid your boss or keep quiet, it is important to address the situation head-on. Start by trying to understand your boss's perspective and the reasons behind their behaviour. Communicating with your boss about how their behaviour is impacting your work and asking for clear guidance can also help you better navigate the situation.

It's important to remember that it's not your responsibility to fix your boss's behaviour, but you can control your reactions and responses to their actions. It's also important to maintain professionalism and avoid reacting emotionally. When faced with an overbearing boss, remaining calm and composed can help you maintain your credibility and professionalism.

The key to dealing with an overbearing boss is to understand what's driving their behaviour. Are they insecure? Do they feel threatened by your competence? Are they under a lot of pressure from higher-ups? Once you understand what's motivating your boss, you can start to develop strategies for managing your interactions with them.

One of the most important things you can do when dealing with an overbearing boss is to set boundaries. Let them know what you need in order to do your job effectively, and don't be afraid to speak up when they're crossing a line. At the same time, it's important to be respectful and professional in your interactions with your boss. Remember, they are still your superior, and it's important to maintain a level of respect even when you disagree with them.

Another important strategy for dealing with an overbearing boss is to focus on building relationships with other people in the workplace. Seek out allies who can offer you support and advice when you're feeling overwhelmed or frustrated. This might mean finding a mentor, joining a professional organization, or simply making friends with your coworkers.

Ultimately, the key to navigating difficult relationships with overbearing bosses is to stay focused on your own goals and priorities. Don't let your boss's behaviour derail your career or your mental health. Instead, stay committed to doing your job to the best of your ability, and seek out support and guidance when you need it.

By adopting the right mindset and implementing effective strategies, you can successfully navigate challenging relationships with overbearing bosses. With persistence and patience, you can learn to communicate more effectively, set boundaries, and manage your emotions in difficult situations. By doing so, you will not only improve your work experience, but also build invaluable skills that will serve you well in all aspects of your professional and personal life. Remember, you have the power to take control of your work environment and thrive despite any obstacles that come your way.

Why Your Office Needs a Pet: The Benefits of Workplace Animals

As our work lives become increasingly stressful and demanding, more and more companies are beginning to realize the benefits of having pets in the workplace. From reducing stress and anxiety to increasing productivity and collaboration, pets can have a positive impact on employees and the workplace as a whole. In this article, we will explore the various benefits of having pets in the workplace and why every office should consider adding a furry friend to the team.

Stress Relief

One of the most well-known benefits of having pets in the workplace is their ability to reduce stress and anxiety. Numerous studies have shown that petting a dog or cat can lower blood pressure and decrease cortisol levels, which is the hormone responsible for stress. Additionally, having a pet in the office can create a more relaxed and comfortable environment, which can help employees feel more at ease and less anxious.

Increased Productivity

Believe it or not, having a pet in the workplace can actually increase productivity. Studies have shown that people who work in offices with pets are more productive and have higher job satisfaction than those who work in pet-free environments. This is likely due to the fact that pets can help reduce stress and increase positive feelings, which in turn can boost motivation and productivity.

Improved Collaboration and Communication

Pets in the workplace can also improve collaboration and communication among employees. Having a pet in the office can create a sense of community and bring people together, which can lead to increased collaboration and better communication. Additionally, pets can act as a conversation starter and provide a common ground for employees to bond over, regardless of their job titles or roles within the company.

Better Health and Well-being

In addition to reducing stress and anxiety, having pets in the workplace can also have a positive impact on employees' overall health and well-being. Studies have shown that people who own pets are generally healthier and happier than those who do not, and having a pet in the office can provide similar benefits. Pets can help employees get more exercise, improve their mental health, and even boost their immune systems.

Increased Employee Retention

Having pets in the workplace can also improve employee retention rates. Employees who feel happy, comfortable, and supported in their work environment are more likely to stay with their current company long-term. By providing a positive and pet-friendly workplace, companies can increase employee satisfaction and reduce turnover rates.

Challenges of Having Pets in the Workplace

While there are many benefits to having pets in the workplace, there are also some challenges that need to be considered. For example, some employees may have allergies or phobias that prevent them from being around certain types of pets. Additionally, pets can be a distraction and require additional attention and care, which can be a challenge for busy employees.

Tips for Successfully Implementing Pets in the Workplace

If you are considering adding pets to your workplace, it is important to do so in a thoughtful and strategic manner. Here are some tips for successfully implementing pets in the workplace:

1. *Set clear guidelines and policies*: Before introducing pets to the workplace, it is important to establish clear guidelines and policies to ensure that everyone is on the same page. This may include rules around pet behaviour, cleanliness, and supervision.

2. *Consider employee preferences*: It is important to take into account the preferences and needs of all employees when deciding what types of pets to allow in the workplace. For example, some people may be more comfortable with cats than dogs, or vice versa.

3. *Address potential challenges*: Be prepared to address potential challenges that may arise when introducing pets to the workplace, such as allergies, phobias, and distractions.

4. *Provide training and support*: Ensure that employees are trained on how to interact with pets in the workplace and that there is proper support in place to care for the animals.

5. *Monitor and evaluate*: Regularly monitor and evaluate the impact of pets on the workplace environment, employee productivity, and overall satisfaction. This will help you identify any issues that may arise and make necessary adjustments to your pet policies and guidelines.

6. *Ensure pet safety*: It is important to prioritize the safety and well-being of both the pets and the employees. Make sure that the workplace is safe for pets and that all necessary precautions are taken to prevent accidents and injuries.

7. *Communicate with clients and visitors*: If your workplace involves regular interactions with clients or visitors, it is important to communicate your pet policies and guidelines to them in advance. This will help to avoid any confusion or discomfort.

8. *Be flexible*: Finally, it is important to be flexible and adaptable when introducing pets to the workplace. Be open to feedback from employees and be willing to make adjustments to your policies and guidelines as needed.

By following these tips, you can successfully introduce pets to your workplace and create a positive and welcoming environment for both employees and pets. However, it is important to remember that not all workplaces are suitable for pets, and you should carefully consider the needs and preferences of your employees before making any decisions.

How to Win Friends and Influence Co-workers: The Art of Networking

In today's fast-paced and highly competitive work environment, it's essential to have strong networking skills. Networking involves building relationships with people within and outside your organization, which can help you gain new opportunities, increase your knowledge, and achieve your professional goals. In this article, we'll discuss the art of networking and provide you with tips on how to win friends and influence co-workers.

Start with a positive attitude.

if you're looking to start networking, the first step is having a positive attitude. You got to be genuinely interested in getting to know people and be willing to put in the time and effort needed to build relationships. To get started, try identifying people you admire or those you can learn from, and approach them with an open mind and willingness to listen.

Networking isn't just about asking for favours or connections; it's about building relationships that are meaningful and mutually beneficial. By approaching people with a positive attitude and a desire to learn from them, you can establish trust and rapport that can lead to more significant opportunities down the road.

Attend events.

Attending events like conferences, workshops, and seminars is a great way to network effectively. These events give you the chance to meet new people, gain knowledge from experts, and share your ideas. Before attending an event, it's important to do your homework by researching the attendees and speakers. Make a list of people you want to meet and topics you want to learn about. Remember to bring along plenty of business cards, so you can easily exchange contact information with people you meet.

Join professional organizations.

When it comes to networking, joining a professional organization related to your field can be a valuable move. It can help you expand your network, stay current with industry trends, and meet other professionals who can offer valuable insights and support.

To make the most of your membership, it's important to take an active role in the organization. Attend meetings regularly, participate in networking events and training sessions, and volunteer for committees or other activities. This can help you build relationships with other members, gain visibility within the organization, and demonstrate your expertise and dedication to your field.

Before joining a professional organization, research different options and choose one that aligns with your interests and goals. Look for an organization that offers opportunities for growth and development, as well as networking opportunities.

Once you've joined, make an effort to get to know other members. Introduce yourself at meetings, attend social events, and take advantage of any mentoring or peer support programs offered by the organization. You can also use social media to connect with other members and stay up-to-date on organization news and events.

Remember, networking is not just about making contacts or getting ahead in your career. It's about building relationships with other professionals who share your interests and goals, and working together to achieve success. By taking an active role in a professional organization, you can expand your network, gain new insights and perspectives, and contribute to the growth and development of your field.

Use social media.

Networking on social media is another effective way to connect with professionals in your field. Platforms like LinkedIn, Twitter, and Facebook offer a great opportunity to expand your network, share your ideas, and learn from others. LinkedIn is especially valuable for networking, as it allows you to create a professional profile, join groups, and connect with people in your industry. To make the most of social media for networking, keep your profiles professional and up-to-date, engage in meaningful conversations with others, and share relevant content. It's also important to remember that social media is a public forum, so be mindful of what you post and how it may reflect on your personal brand.

Attend informational interviews.

Informational interviews are a great way to learn about different companies and industries and meet new people. An informational interview involves meeting with someone who works in a field or industry you are interested in, and asking them questions about their job, career path, and experiences. This type of interview can help you gain valuable insights, and also allows you to network with someone who may be able to provide you with additional contacts or job opportunities.

Follow up.

It's crucial to follow up after meeting someone to build a successful network. Sending a personalized email or note after meeting someone, thanking them for their time and expressing your interest in keeping in touch, is important. If you promised to send them additional information or connect them with someone else, make sure to follow through. Regularly staying in touch with your contacts can help you build long-lasting relationships.

When following up with your contacts, be sure to be genuine and thoughtful. Don't send generic emails or messages that seem like you copied and pasted them. Make it clear that you remember who they are and what you talked about, and show that you value the connection. It's also essential to be respectful of their time and not overdo it with follow-up messages. If you don't hear back from them, don't be discouraged. People are busy, and it doesn't necessarily mean they're not interested in keeping in touch. Just be patient and keep networking.

Be helpful.

Networking is not just about receiving help from others, but also giving back. When you meet someone new, think about how you can assist them in achieving their goals, whether it's by introducing them to someone in your network or providing them with valuable advice. Being helpful can build a good relationship between you and others in your professional community. Remember that networking is a two-way street, and you must be willing to help others as much as you expect them to help you.

By providing assistance to others, you can develop a good reputation in your professional network. You become a valuable asset to others, and they will more likely remember you when opportunities arise. However, it's essential to ensure that the assistance you provide is genuine and not just for the sake of getting something in return.

Building relationships based on mutual assistance is crucial for successful networking. Don't just focus on what others can do for you, but also on what you can do for them. This way, you create a positive impression of yourself, and others in your network will be more likely to remember you when opportunities arise.

Networking is a crucial part of building a successful career. By developing your networking skills, you can expand your knowledge, gain new opportunities, and build long-lasting relationships. Start by adopting a positive attitude, attending events, joining professional organizations, using social media, attending informational interviews, following up, and being helpful. With these tips, you can master the art of networking and win friends and influence co-workers.

Why a Clean Office is a Productive Office: The Importance of Cleanliness

A clean office is not only a pleasant environment to work in but also an essential factor in ensuring the productivity and overall well-being of employees. A dirty, cluttered office can negatively impact the morale and productivity of employees, while a clean and organized office can increase efficiency and employee satisfaction. In this article, we will explore the importance of cleanliness in the workplace, the benefits of maintaining a clean office, and tips on how to keep your office clean and organized.

Importance of Cleanliness in the Workplace:

1. **Health and Safety**: One of the primary reasons why cleanliness is important in the workplace is for the health and safety of employees. A clean office reduces the risk of germs and bacteria that can lead to illness and absenteeism. It also helps to prevent accidents and

injuries, such as slips, trips, and falls, that can occur when the workspace is cluttered and disorganized.

2. **Increased Productivity**: A clean and organized workspace can help to increase productivity by reducing distractions and creating a more focused and efficient work environment. Employees are less likely to waste time looking for lost documents or items, and a clean workspace can also help to reduce stress and increase motivation.

3. **Positive Image**: A clean and well-maintained office gives a positive image of the company to clients and visitors. It demonstrates that the company cares about its employees, their well-being, and the environment they work in.

Benefits of Maintaining a Clean Office:

1. **Improved Air Quality**: A clean office means better air quality, which can lead to improved health and productivity. Dust, pollen, and other allergens can accumulate in an unclean office, leading to respiratory problems and allergies. A clean office also reduces the number of germs and bacteria that can spread and cause illness.

2. **Increased Employee Morale**: A clean office creates a more positive and uplifting environment, leading to increased employee morale. Employees are more likely to feel valued and respected, leading to greater job satisfaction and increased productivity.

3. **Reduced Stress**: A cluttered and disorganized workspace can cause stress and anxiety for employees. A clean and organized workspace reduces stress levels, leading to improved mental health and greater productivity.

Tips for Keeping Your Office Clean and Organized:

1. **Develop a Cleaning Routine**: Establish a cleaning routine for the office, including regular cleaning of surfaces, equipment, and floors. Set aside time each day or week to complete cleaning tasks and assign responsibilities to employees to ensure that the office is clean and organized.

2. **Get Rid of Clutter**: Remove any unnecessary items from the workspace, including old files and equipment that are no longer needed. Decluttering the workspace can create more space and reduce distractions, leading to increased productivity.

3. **Encourage Employees to Keep Their Workspace Clean**: Encourage employees to keep their workspace clean and organized by providing storage solutions and reminding them of the importance of maintaining a clean workspace. Consider setting up a reward system for employees who maintain a clean workspace, such as a gift card or extra vacation day.

4. **Provide Cleaning Supplies**: Provide cleaning supplies such as disinfectant wipes, paper towels, and garbage bags to encourage employees to clean up after themselves. This can help to prevent the build-up of dirt and clutter in the office.

A clean and organized office is essential for the productivity, health, and well-being of employees. By maintaining a clean workspace, businesses can reduce the risk of illness, increase employee morale, and create a more positive and efficient work environment. Follow these tips for keeping your office clean and organized, and enjoy the benefits of a clean and productive workspace.

How to Be Assertive Without Being Aggressive: Standing Up for Yourself in the Workplace

Effective communication is key to success in the workplace. However, many people struggle to communicate their needs and boundaries effectively. They may find themselves either being too passive and unable to stand up for themselves or being too aggressive and disregarding the needs and feelings of others. The key is to find the balance between assertiveness and aggressiveness.

Assertiveness is a communication style that involves expressing yourself in a clear, confident, and direct manner while still respecting the needs and opinions of others. It involves being able to communicate your thoughts, feelings, and needs without coming across as hostile or aggressive. Assertive communication allows you to stand up for yourself and advocate for your needs, without violating the rights of others.

On the other hand, aggressiveness is a communication style that involves forcing your will upon others without regard for their feelings or needs. This approach may involve bullying, intimidation, and hostile behaviour. Aggressive communication can create a hostile work environment and damage relationships with colleagues, clients, and superiors.

Finding the balance between assertiveness and aggressiveness is crucial for effective communication in the workplace. Assertive communication allows you to express your needs and boundaries while maintaining respect for others. It involves clear and direct communication that is free from personal attacks or hostility. Assertive communication can help you build stronger relationships with colleagues, promote collaboration, and improve productivity.

In contrast, aggressive communication can lead to conflicts, misunderstandings, and mistrust. It can create a toxic work environment that undermines teamwork, productivity, and morale. Aggressive communication may give you a sense of power and control in the short term, but it can damage your reputation and limit your long-term success.

To be an effective communicator in the workplace, you need to find the balance between assertiveness and aggressiveness. You need to be able to communicate your needs and boundaries in a clear and direct manner, while also respecting the needs and opinions of others. You need to be confident in your abilities, but also open to feedback and willing to collaborate with others. With practice, you can develop a communication style that is assertive, effective, and respectful of others.

Here are some tips on how to be assertive without being aggressive in the workplace:

- **Speak up, but listen too**: When you have something to say, don't hesitate to speak up. But make sure to also listen to others and take their opinions into account. Assertiveness involves finding a middle ground where you express your own needs and ideas while also being open to other perspectives.

- **Use "I" statements**: Instead of placing blame or making accusations, focus on your own thoughts and feelings. For example, instead of saying "You never listen to me," try saying "I feel frustrated when I don't feel heard." This makes the conversation about your own experience rather than attacking the other person.

- **Be specific**: When giving feedback or making a request, be as specific as possible. This helps to avoid misunderstandings and ensures that everyone is on the same page. Instead of saying "I need more help from you," try saying "Can you please take over the weekly report for me so that I can focus on other projects?"

- **Use a neutral tone**: Avoid using a confrontational or accusatory tone when speaking with others. Instead, try to remain calm and neutral in your tone. This helps to keep the conversation productive and focused on finding solutions rather than placing blame.

- **Practice active listening**: When someone else is speaking, make sure to actively listen and show that you understand their perspective. This helps to build trust and respect in the conversation, and can help to prevent misunderstandings or conflicts from arising.

- **Know when to walk away**: Sometimes, despite our best efforts, we may encounter someone who is unwilling to listen or compromise. In these situations, it's important to know when to walk away and take a break. This doesn't mean giving up, but rather taking time to regroup and come back to the conversation with a fresh perspective.

- **Be open to feedback**: Being assertive also means being open to feedback and willing to make changes. If someone offers you feedback, take it as an opportunity to learn and grow rather than as a criticism. Remember, constructive feedback can help you become a better communicator and ultimately a more effective team member.

In conclusion, being assertive in the workplace is essential to achieve success, but it is equally important to maintain a balance between being assertive and aggressive. The key is to learn effective communication skills that enable you to express your needs and boundaries clearly and confidently, while also respecting the needs and opinions of others. By practicing these tips, you can develop assertiveness in the workplace without crossing the line into aggressiveness.

Effective communication not only helps you to express yourself but also to build stronger relationships with your co-workers.

When you communicate effectively, you establish trust and credibility with your colleagues, which can lead to greater collaboration and teamwork. Moreover, building strong relationships with your co-workers can also help you to advance your career by providing you with valuable networking opportunities and increasing your chances of receiving promotions or other career advancement opportunities.

In addition, by being assertive, you can ensure that your voice is heard, and your ideas are valued. You will be able to contribute more effectively to team projects and collaborate more meaningfully with others. This will not only help you to achieve greater success in your career but also make a positive impact on the overall success of your organization.

Overall, finding the balance between assertiveness and aggressiveness is crucial for achieving success in the workplace. By following the tips outlined in this article, you can develop the skills necessary to communicate assertively, build strong relationships with your co-workers, and ultimately achieve your career goals.

Why Work/Life Balance is Essential: The Art of Taking Time Off

In today's society, finding a work-life balance can be quite a challenge, especially in the fast-paced and demanding modern workplace. Many individuals struggle to balance the demands of their professional life with their personal responsibilities, which can lead to stress, anxiety, and even burnout. Achieving work/life balance is essential for maintaining physical and mental health, and it can also lead to improved productivity, job satisfaction, and overall happiness.

The consequences of not achieving a work/life balance can be detrimental to both individuals and their employers. Employees who are overworked and stressed are more likely to experience health problems, decreased productivity, and higher rates of absenteeism. This can lead to increased healthcare costs and decreased profitability for companies. On the other hand, organizations that prioritize work/life balance for their employees can attract and retain top talent, improve employee morale and engagement, and ultimately, achieve greater success.

Why Work/Life Balance is Essential

Work/life balance is essential for physical and mental well-being, and it can help increase productivity and job satisfaction. Here are some reasons why work/life balance is essential:

1. **Reduces Stress**: One of the main reasons why work/life balance is essential is because it helps to reduce stress. When we work long hours and don't take time to relax and recharge, we become stressed, which can lead to burnout and even depression.

2. **Increases Productivity**: Taking time off work and achieving work/life balance can help increase productivity. When we're well-rested and have time to pursue hobbies and other interests, we come back to work with renewed energy and focus.

3. **Improves Physical Health**: Work/life balance can help improve physical health. When we have time to exercise and eat healthy meals, we're less likely to get sick or develop chronic health conditions.

4. **Enhances Relationships**: Work/life balance can also enhance our relationships. When we have time to spend with family and friends, we strengthen those relationships, which can provide emotional support during stressful times.

Tips on How to Achieve Work/Life Balance

Achieving work/life balance can be challenging, but it's essential for physical and mental well-being. Here are some tips on how to achieve work/life balance:

1. **Set Boundaries**: It's essential to set boundaries between work and personal time. This can include avoiding checking work emails or taking work calls during personal time, and setting specific work hours.

2. **Take Time Off**: Taking time off work is essential to achieve work/life balance. This can include taking vacations, personal days, or even mental health days to recharge and relax.

3. **Prioritize Hobbies and Interests**: Prioritizing hobbies and interests outside of work can help achieve work/life balance. This can include activities like exercising, reading, or pursuing creative projects.

4. **Practice Self-Care**: Practicing self-care is essential for achieving work/life balance. This can include activities like meditation, getting enough sleep, and eating healthy meals.

5. **Learn to Say No**: Learning to say no to additional work projects or requests for your time is important for achieving work/life balance. It's okay to prioritize personal time and set boundaries.

In conclusion, work/life balance is crucial for personal and professional fulfillment. It's essential to prioritize self-care, set boundaries, take time off work, and engage in hobbies and interests outside of work to achieve balance. By doing so, individuals can reduce stress and burnout, improve overall health and well-being, and increase job satisfaction and productivity. It's also important to learn to say no to excessive work demands and prioritize self-care. Remember that achieving work/life balance is not only beneficial for your personal well-being but also for your work performance and career success. In today's fast-paced work environment, it's easy to get caught up in the constant pressure to work more, but taking time off work is not a luxury. It's a necessity that helps individuals recharge, gain perspective, and come back to work refreshed and ready to tackle challenges. By implementing these tips and prioritizing work/life balance, individuals can create a more fulfilling and sustainable work and personal life. So, take the time to prioritize your well-being, set boundaries, and find a healthy balance between work and life.

Why You Should Always Be Learning: The Importance of Professional Development

The need for ongoing professional development has become increasingly important in today's fast-paced and dynamic job market. In order to stay competitive, individuals must continuously seek out opportunities to enhance their skills, knowledge, and abilities. With the rapid pace of technological advancements and the ever-changing business landscape, it is imperative that professionals remain up-to-date on the latest developments in their field.

Professional development can take many forms, including attending conferences and workshops, pursuing additional education or certifications, seeking out mentorship and coaching, and engaging in self-directed learning. By taking a proactive approach to professional development, individuals can stay ahead of the curve and position themselves for success in their careers.

For those just starting out in their careers, professional development is especially critical. It is important to establish a solid foundation of skills and knowledge early on in order to build a strong professional network and advance in the field. Pursuing internships, volunteering, and seeking out mentorship opportunities are all valuable ways to gain experience and develop skills.

However, professional development is not just important for those starting out in their careers. Even seasoned professionals can benefit from ongoing learning and development. As industries and technologies continue to evolve, professionals must adapt and expand their skill sets in order to remain competitive. Pursuing additional education or certifications, attending conferences, and engaging in self-directed learning are all effective ways for experienced professionals to stay up-to-date and relevant in their field.

Ultimately, ongoing professional development is crucial for success in the modern workforce. By staying informed, continuously learning, and adapting to new developments, individuals can position themselves for growth and advancement in their careers. It is important to recognize that professional development is not a one-time event, but rather a lifelong journey. By prioritizing ongoing learning and development, individuals can build a fulfilling and successful career.

So why exactly should you make professional development a priority? Let's take a closer look at some of the key reasons.

Stay Relevant in Your Industry

In today's fast-paced and constantly changing job market, ongoing professional development is crucial for individuals at all stages of their careers. The world is changing rapidly, and new technologies and practices are being introduced every day. For professionals to remain competitive and relevant in their fields, it's essential to keep up with the latest trends and best practices.

One way to stay current with industry changes and advancements is by taking advantage of professional development opportunities. Workshops, conferences, and online courses are just a few examples of the many learning opportunities available to professionals. These opportunities provide individuals with the chance to learn new skills, stay up-to-date with the latest trends, and connect with other professionals in their field.

By participating in professional development opportunities, individuals can stay on top of the latest developments in their field, enabling them to better handle new challenges and opportunities as they arise. As technology continues to evolve, many industries are undergoing significant changes. New tools and techniques are being introduced, and old practices are becoming obsolete. Professionals who don't keep up with these changes risk falling behind and becoming less competitive in the job market.

Professional development is particularly important for individuals who are just starting their careers. The job market is becoming increasingly competitive, and employers are looking for candidates who have the latest skills and knowledge. By investing in professional development, young professionals can acquire the skills they need to stand out in the job market and succeed in their careers.

But professional development is not just for new professionals. Experienced professionals also need to continue learning to remain competitive and relevant. With technology and industry practices changing so rapidly, there is always something new to learn. By staying up to date with the latest trends and practices, experienced professionals can continue to grow and thrive in their careers.

In addition to providing individuals with the latest skills and knowledge, professional development opportunities can also help professionals connect with other like-minded individuals. Workshops and conferences provide opportunities for professionals to network and make new connections. These connections can be valuable for career advancement, as well as for finding new opportunities in the job market.

In conclusion, professional development is essential for individuals at all stages of their careers. By investing in ongoing learning and development opportunities, individuals can stay current with industry trends and best practices. This, in turn, can help them stay competitive and relevant in the job market, increase their job satisfaction, and open up new opportunities for career growth and advancement.

Advance Your Career

Professional development is a valuable investment that can pay dividends in terms of career advancement and job prospects. As you enhance your skills and knowledge, you become a more valuable asset to your current organization. You can perform your current role more effectively and efficiently, and take on additional responsibilities with confidence. This increased competency can help you stand out from your peers and make you a strong candidate for promotion.

Moreover, professional development can help you expand your career options by opening up new avenues for growth and opportunity. If you are looking to transition to a new industry or role, continuing education can help you develop the necessary skills and expertise to make the switch. Employers are often impressed by candidates who are committed to their own development, and investing in your own growth can help you differentiate yourself from other job applicants.

Continuing education and professional development can also help you stay up-to-date with emerging trends and best practices in your industry. As technology and practices evolve, it's crucial to remain current and competitive. By staying on top of the latest developments in your field, you'll be better prepared to tackle new challenges and capitalize on emerging opportunities.

In summary, professional development can help you advance in your current role, broaden your career options, and stay current with the latest trends and practices in your industry. By investing in your own growth and development, you can enhance your value as an employee and position yourself for long-term career success.

Boost Your Confidence

Engaging in professional development can have a positive impact on one's confidence and well-being. As individuals acquire new skills and knowledge, they can feel more capable and confident in their abilities. This can translate into better job performance, leading to increased job satisfaction. Additionally, professional development can help individuals overcome imposter syndrome or self-doubt by providing them with evidence of their competence and expertise.

Attending workshops, seminars, or conferences, or enrolling in online courses, can help individuals gain new knowledge and skills relevant to their industry or job. With increased knowledge, individuals can apply new techniques and strategies in their work, leading to a sense of accomplishment and fulfillment. Moreover, continuing education can provide individuals with opportunities to connect with like-minded individuals and form professional relationships that may lead to new career opportunities or collaborations.

Furthermore, professional development can help individuals identify and pursue their career goals. Through training and education, individuals can gain a better understanding of their industry, including emerging trends and technologies. This can help individuals identify areas where they may want to specialize or develop expertise, setting them on a path towards their career goals. Additionally, professional development can help individuals identify and address any gaps in their skills or knowledge that may be hindering their career growth.

In summary, professional development can be an excellent way to boost confidence, improve job satisfaction, and identify and pursue career goals. By engaging in ongoing learning and skill-building, individuals can become more valuable assets to their organizations and better equipped to handle new challenges and opportunities. Moreover, continuing education can provide opportunities for networking and collaboration, leading to potential career growth and advancement.

Expand Your Network

Engaging in professional development activities can also broaden your professional network, which can provide various benefits. By attending workshops, conferences, or other events, you can meet and connect with other professionals in your field, potentially leading to new opportunities and relationships. Expanding your professional network can be advantageous in several ways, including learning about new job openings, receiving advice or mentorship from experienced professionals, and exchanging knowledge and ideas through collaboration.

Meeting new professionals in your industry can give you a better understanding of the current state of your field and help you keep up with the latest trends and innovations. It can also provide you with a fresh perspective and insights on how to tackle challenges or problems that you may be facing in your job. Networking can also lead to potential partnerships and collaborations that can enhance your work and bring new ideas and approaches to your organization.

Additionally, expanding your network can also help you establish a positive reputation and build your personal brand in your industry. Through networking, you can develop a reputation for being knowledgeable, helpful, and collaborative, which can make you an attractive candidate for new opportunities and potential employers. As you establish yourself as a valuable member of your professional community, you may be approached with job opportunities or projects that you wouldn't have otherwise known about.

In summary, professional development is not only about building skills and knowledge but also about building connections and expanding your professional network. Attending events and networking with other professionals can lead to new opportunities, partnerships, and collaborations, while also improving your reputation in your industry. By investing in your professional development, you can enhance your career prospects and achieve greater success and satisfaction in your work.

Learn New Perspectives

Engaging in professional development can broaden your perspectives and introduce you to new ways of thinking. By attending workshops, webinars, or reading industry publications, you can expose yourself to different viewpoints and techniques that can help you innovate in your work. Learning from experts in your field can challenge your preconceived notions and inspire you to find new solutions to old problems. Additionally, attending training sessions or conferences can offer a fresh perspective on current trends and developments in your industry, keeping you up-to-date with the latest advances.

Moreover, gaining a new perspective can also help you see your work in a different light, leading to increased job satisfaction and motivation. When you are constantly learning, you are more likely to feel engaged in your work, and be eager to take on new challenges. This can lead to a more fulfilling career and a sense of accomplishment, which can have a positive impact on your mental health and overall well-being.

Finally, acquiring new perspectives through professional development can help you become a more valuable asset to your organization. Bringing fresh ideas and innovative approaches to your work can lead to increased efficiency, productivity, and profitability. Employers appreciate employees who are proactive in learning and growing in their field, and who can apply their new knowledge and skills to benefit the company. Therefore, investing in your professional development can not only benefit you personally, but it can also have a positive impact on your organization as a whole.

Keep Your Brain Active

Professional development can be an enjoyable way to keep your mind active and engaged. Learning new skills and knowledge is a lifelong pursuit that can provide personal fulfillment and satisfaction. As you challenge yourself to grow and develop professionally, you'll also keep your brain sharp, which can have positive effects on your overall well-being.

When you engage in professional development, you may find that you enjoy learning more than you ever thought possible. You may discover new areas of interest or explore topics that you never considered before. This can lead to a sense of personal satisfaction and enjoyment that can spill over into other areas of your life.

Additionally, professional development can provide a break from the monotony of everyday work life. Attending conferences or participating in workshops can offer a change of pace and a chance to interact with new people. This can be a refreshing break from the routine of daily work tasks.

Finally, professional development can be a way to stay engaged and curious about the world around you. As you learn about new topics and acquire new skills, you may find yourself more interested in current events, scientific discoveries, and cultural trends. This can lead to a greater sense of connection to the world and a deeper appreciation for the complexities of the world we live in.

In conclusion, professional development is an essential component of a successful and fulfilling career. By continually building your skills and knowledge, you'll stay relevant in your industry, advance your career, boost your confidence, expand your network, learn new perspectives, and keep your brain active. So whether you're just starting out in your career or have been in the workforce for years, don't hesitate to take advantage of professional development opportunities to help you grow and succeed.

Why a Sense of Humour is the Best Tool in Your Work Toolbox: Laughter in the Workplace

The workplace can often be a challenging environment, filled with high-pressure deadlines, demanding clients, and stressful situations. However, research has shown that incorporating humour into the workplace can have a positive impact on both employees and employers. Laughter has been found to help reduce stress and anxiety, boost morale, and increase productivity.

When employees are stressed, their productivity and motivation can suffer, which can have negative consequences for the organization. However, laughter can help reduce stress levels and create a more positive work environment. When people laugh, it triggers the release of endorphins, which are natural feel-good chemicals that can help reduce stress and improve mood. Additionally, laughter can help build stronger relationships between colleagues and foster a sense of camaraderie.

Incorporating humour into the workplace can take many forms, from telling jokes and sharing funny stories to organizing team-building activities that involve laughter. It's important to keep in mind that humour should always be appropriate and respectful, and should never come at the expense of someone else.

One way to incorporate humour into the workplace is through office pranks or light-hearted jokes. However, it's important to ensure that these pranks are done in good taste and do not cross the line into inappropriate or offensive behaviour. Another way to incorporate humour is by holding team-building activities that involve laughter, such as a comedy show or improv workshop.

It's important to note that humour should never be used as a way to mask serious issues or avoid dealing with difficult situations. While laughter can be a helpful tool for reducing stress and improving morale, it should not be used as a substitute for addressing important workplace issues.

In addition to its positive effects on workplace morale and productivity, laughter can also have physical and mental health benefits. Research has shown that laughter can help lower blood pressure, reduce the risk of heart disease, and boost the immune system. Additionally, laughter has been found to be an effective tool for reducing symptoms of depression and anxiety.

So, incorporating humour into the workplace can have numerous benefits for both employees and employers. It can help reduce stress, boost morale, and increase productivity, while also fostering stronger relationships between colleagues. However, it's important to ensure that humour is always appropriate and respectful, and that it does not distract from important workplace issues. By incorporating humour in a thoughtful and intentional way, workplaces can create a more positive and engaging environment for their employees.

Benefits of Laughter in the Workplace

1. Relieves Stress and Tension

Workplace stress is a major concern that can negatively impact an individual's physical and mental health, as well as their overall productivity. Laughter, on the other hand, is an effective and natural way to relieve stress and promote relaxation. By incorporating humour into the workplace, individuals can help alleviate tension and make challenging situations seem more manageable.

Studies have shown that laughter releases endorphins, which are natural chemicals in the body that promote feelings of pleasure and well-being. Laughter also decreases the levels of stress hormones like cortisol and adrenaline, which can have negative effects on the body when produced in excess. By promoting feelings of relaxation and reducing stress hormones, laughter can improve overall health and well-being.

Furthermore, laughter can help individuals gain perspective on challenging situations in the workplace. It can provide a moment of relief from the stresses of the job and help individuals maintain a positive attitude even when faced with difficult tasks. This positive attitude can in turn enhance productivity and job satisfaction.

2. Boosts Morale and Teamwork

Laughter is an essential ingredient for creating a positive and enjoyable work environment, which can improve morale and promote teamwork. When employees are in a good mood, they are more likely to collaborate and support each other, leading to more productive and efficient work. Laughter can also break down communication barriers and foster a sense of community among colleagues. By encouraging humor and laughter in the workplace, organizations can create a positive culture that values fun and happiness alongside hard work and professionalism.

3. Enhances Creativity and Innovation

In addition to its stress-reducing and team-building benefits, humour can also have a positive impact on creativity and innovation in the workplace. When individuals feel relaxed and at ease, they are more likely to let their guard down and think more creatively. Humour can create a more open and accepting environment where employees feel comfortable sharing their ideas without fear of judgement or criticism.

Furthermore, incorporating humour into brainstorming sessions or team meetings can help break down mental barriers and encourage individuals to think outside the box. Playful and humorous approaches to problem-solving can lead to more innovative solutions and improve work processes. Humour can also help individuals maintain a positive outlook when facing challenges or setbacks, which can contribute to more resilient and adaptable teams.

4. Improves Communication and Collaboration

Laughter can play a crucial role in promoting better communication and collaboration in the workplace. When people share a laugh, it creates a sense of camaraderie and breaks down barriers. Humor can also promote open and honest communication, which is crucial for effective collaboration. When people feel comfortable and relaxed, they are more likely to share their ideas and perspectives openly, leading to better problem-solving and decision-making. Furthermore, humor can help people to better understand each other's perspectives and build trust, leading to stronger working relationships. Ultimately, promoting laughter and humor in the workplace can lead to better communication and collaboration, which can translate to improved job satisfaction and productivity.

Tips for Incorporating Humour into the Workplace

1. Be Yourself

Humour is personal, so it's important to be true to yourself when incorporating it into your work life. Don't try to be someone you're not or force humour that doesn't come naturally to you. Find your own style of humour and use it to create a positive and fun workplace culture.

2. Know Your Audience

While humour is personal, it's also important to consider your audience. What may be funny to one person may not be funny to another. Consider your colleagues' personalities, interests, and cultural backgrounds when incorporating humour into your work life.

3. Use Humour Appropriately

Humour can be a powerful tool, but it can also be inappropriate if used in the wrong context. Avoid using humour that is offensive, insensitive, or discriminatory. Use humour to create a positive and inclusive workplace culture, not to belittle or offend others.

4. Keep it Professional.

While humour can be a great way to boost morale and create a fun workplace culture, it's important to keep it professional. Avoid using humour that is inappropriate for the workplace or that undermines the seriousness of the work being done. Keep in mind that humour should enhance productivity, not distract from it.

5. Don't Force It

Humour should come naturally and be used sparingly. Don't try to force humour or use it excessively. Use humour to lighten the mood or to inject a bit of fun into the workplace, but don't use it as a crutch or as a way to avoid serious issues.

Laughter is a powerful tool that can enhance productivity, boost morale, and create a positive and fun workplace culture. Incorporating humour into your work life can help alleviate stress, promote teamwork, stimulate creativity, and improve communication. By being yourself, knowing your audience, using humour appropriately, keeping it professional, and not forcing it, you can use humour to enhance your work life and achieve greater success in the workplace.

How to Deal With a Micromanaging Boss: A Guide to Keeping Your Sanity

Micromanagement in the workplace is a serious problem that can negatively impact both employees and their organizations. It is a sign of a lack of trust and can lead to stress, frustration, and low morale among employees. A micromanaging boss can make it difficult for employees to feel valued, respected, and empowered in their roles, which can ultimately lead to decreased productivity and even turnover. However, there are ways to address this issue and maintain your sanity in the process.

Understand the root cause of the micromanaging behaviour.

Micromanaging behaviour can create tension and a lack of trust between employees and their bosses. Understanding the underlying cause of this behaviour can help you navigate the situation with more ease. The reasons behind micromanaging can be multifaceted, but they usually revolve around a lack of trust or a need for control.

It's essential to observe your boss's behaviour and try to understand the source of their behaviour. For example, is your boss experiencing anxiety about the outcome of a project? Are they worried about meeting a deadline? Or do they feel the need to be involved in every decision? By recognizing the root cause, you can tailor your approach to the specific situation.

Once you have identified the root cause, approach the situation with empathy and understanding. If your boss is anxious about a project, offer support and reassurance that you will do your best to ensure its success. If your boss feels the need to be involved in every decision, ask them to clarify their expectations and work with them to establish clear boundaries for decision-making.

It's important to keep in mind that micromanaging behaviour may also be a result of a lack of communication. Make sure you are communicating regularly with your boss and keeping them updated on your progress. This can help build trust and reduce the need for micromanaging.

Another helpful approach is to establish clear goals and expectations with your boss. By setting goals together, you can ensure that you are working towards the same objectives, and your boss can feel confident that you are on track. This can help reduce the need for constant oversight and micromanaging.

It's also important to maintain a positive attitude and stay focused on the task at hand. Micromanagement can be stressful and frustrating, but it's crucial to stay focused on the work and not let the behaviour of your boss distract you. Remember to stay professional and respectful, even if the situation becomes challenging.

In conclusion, understanding the root cause of micromanaging behaviour can help you navigate the situation more effectively. By approaching the situation with empathy and clear communication, you can build trust and establish clear expectations with your boss. Remember to stay positive, focused, and professional, even in challenging situations.

Communicate effectively with your boss.

Effective communication is key to dealing with a micromanaging boss. While it may be tempting to avoid communication altogether, it's important to keep your boss in the loop about your work to build trust and confidence. Clear and consistent communication can help ease your boss's need for control and provide them with the information they need to feel secure about the outcome of a project.

Start by being clear about your goals and timelines. This will help your boss understand what you are working on and when they can expect results. Set specific and achievable targets for your work, and make sure your boss knows what they are. Provide regular updates on your progress and be transparent about any issues or roadblocks you encounter. This will help your boss feel like they are part of the process without feeling the need to micromanage.

When communicating with a micromanaging boss, it's important to be assertive and set boundaries. If your boss is constantly checking in with you, politely remind them that you have everything under control and will update them when necessary. Be firm but polite, and try to keep the conversation positive and productive. Use active listening skills to understand your boss's concerns and respond with empathy.

It's also important to communicate your own needs and concerns. If you feel overwhelmed or stressed by your boss's micromanaging behaviour, let them know how it is affecting you and your work. Be clear about what you need from your boss in terms of support and guidance, and ask for their input on how to improve your work. By communicating your needs and concerns, you can build a more constructive and supportive relationship with your boss.

Additionally, if you find that your boss's micromanaging behaviour is negatively impacting your productivity or mental health, it may be necessary to have a more serious conversation. Approach the situation calmly and professionally, and be prepared to provide specific examples of how their behaviour is affecting you and your work. Focus on finding solutions and alternatives that will allow you to work more independently while still meeting your boss's needs.

In summary, effective communication is essential for dealing with a micromanaging boss. Be clear about your goals and progress, but also be assertive and set boundaries when necessary. Communicate your own needs and concerns, and be open to finding solutions that work for both you and your boss. By building a constructive and supportive relationship, you can ease your boss's need for control and create a more productive and positive work environment.

Build trust with your boss.

Dealing with a micromanaging boss can be a challenge, but building trust with your boss can help alleviate this behaviour. Micromanaging behaviour often stems from a lack of trust, so taking the time to build a strong relationship with your boss can be an effective strategy for reducing micromanagement.

To build trust with your boss, it's important to be consistent, reliable, and transparent in your work. This means meeting deadlines, communicating regularly, and following through on your commitments. When your boss sees that you are dependable and capable of handling your responsibilities, he or she may be more likely to let go of the need to micromanage.

It's also important to be honest and transparent with your boss. If there are issues that need to be addressed or if you need more support in your work, speak up and let your boss know. By being open and honest, you can build a stronger relationship with your boss based on trust and mutual respect.

Another way to build trust with your boss is to offer solutions instead of just identifying problems. If you encounter a problem, think of potential solutions before bringing it to your boss's attention. This will demonstrate your problem-solving skills and your commitment to finding solutions.

In addition, it's important to maintain a positive attitude and a willingness to learn. Show your boss that you are dedicated to your job and that you are willing to take on new challenges. This will help to build your boss's confidence in your abilities and may reduce the need for micromanagement.

Lastly, it's important to be patient. Building trust takes time, and it may take some time for your boss to let go of micromanaging behaviour. However, by consistently demonstrating your capabilities and your commitment to your work, you can help to create a more trusting and collaborative working relationship with your boss.

In conclusion, building trust with your boss is a key strategy for dealing with a micromanaging boss. By being consistent, reliable, transparent, and open, you can build a strong relationship with your boss based on trust and mutual respect. This can lead to a more positive work environment and can help to reduce micromanagement behaviour.

Take ownership of your work

Taking ownership of your work is an important aspect of being a successful employee, especially if you are dealing with a micromanaging boss. When you take ownership of your work, you become more proactive and less reactive. You are better able to manage your workload, set priorities, and meet deadlines. Additionally, taking ownership can help to build trust with your boss, which can ultimately lead to a reduction in micromanaging behaviour.

One way to take ownership of your work is to be proactive. This means anticipating problems, coming up with solutions, and taking action before being asked. For example, if you know that a project deadline is approaching, you can take the initiative to check in with your team members, review the project status, and identify any potential roadblocks. By doing so, you are taking ownership of the project and demonstrating your commitment to its success.

Another way to take ownership of your work is to take responsibility for your tasks and projects. This means being accountable for the work you do and accepting the consequences of your actions. For example, if you make a mistake, own up to it and take steps to rectify the situation. By taking responsibility, you show your boss that you are capable of handling your responsibilities and that you can be trusted to get the job done.

It's also important to be self-motivated when taking ownership of your work. This means setting goals, creating a plan to achieve them, and tracking your progress. By being self-motivated, you are less likely to need constant direction and supervision from your boss. Instead, you can work independently and efficiently, which can help to reduce micromanaging behaviour.

Another aspect of taking ownership of your work is being proactive in seeking feedback. Don't wait for your boss to provide feedback; instead, ask for it proactively. This shows that you are open to constructive criticism and that you are committed to improving your work. Additionally, seeking feedback can help to identify areas where you can improve, which can help to reduce micromanaging behaviour in the long run.

Finally, taking ownership of your work means being accountable for your own development. This means seeking out opportunities for growth, such as attending training sessions, seeking mentorship, or taking on new responsibilities. By doing so, you demonstrate to your boss that you are committed to improving your skills and knowledge, which can help to reduce micromanaging behaviour by showing that you are capable of handling more responsibility.

In conclusion, taking ownership of your work is a powerful tool in dealing with a micromanaging boss. By being proactive, taking responsibility, being self-motivated, seeking feedback, and being accountable for your own development, you can demonstrate to your boss that you are capable of handling your responsibilities and that you can be trusted to get the job done. This can help to reduce micromanaging behaviour and create a more productive and positive work environment.

Stay positive.

Dealing with a micromanaging boss can cause a great deal of stress and frustration, but maintaining a positive attitude is crucial. Instead of complaining or venting to your colleagues about your boss, focus on the things that you can control. Concentrate on your work, maintain your professionalism, and continue to perform to the best of your abilities. A positive attitude will help you to stay motivated and focused, and can also have a positive impact on the morale of your colleagues. If you find that you are struggling to stay positive, consider taking breaks throughout the day to clear your mind and refocus your energy. Whether it is taking a walk outside or practicing meditation, find ways to recharge yourself and stay motivated. Remember that while you may not be able to control your boss's behaviour, you can control how you respond to it. By staying positive and focusing on the things you can control, you can maintain your professionalism and continue to excel in your work.

In conclusion, dealing with a micromanaging boss can be challenging, but it is possible to manage the situation effectively. By understanding the root cause of the behaviour, communicating effectively, building trust, and taking ownership of your work, you can alleviate the micromanaging behaviour and establish a more productive and positive working relationship with your boss. Remember to stay positive, focus on the things you can control, and seek support from trusted colleagues or mentors if needed. By taking these steps, you can not only improve your own job satisfaction but also create a more harmonious and effective work environment for yourself and your colleagues.

Why You Shouldn't Fear Failure: Learning From Mistakes in the Workplace

Failure is often seen as a negative experience in the workplace. Many people fear it and do their best to avoid it, but the truth is that failure can be a valuable learning experience that can help you grow both personally and professionally. In this article, we'll explore the reasons why you shouldn't fear failure and the lessons that can be learned from it.

First and foremost, it's important to understand that failure is a natural part of the learning process. In fact, some of the world's most successful people have experienced failure at some point in their lives. Steve Jobs was fired from Apple, Walt Disney was fired by a newspaper editor for lacking imagination and having no good ideas, and Oprah Winfrey was fired from her job as a TV news anchor. But each of these individuals used their failures as a stepping stone to success.

One of the reasons why failure can be so valuable is that it helps you to develop resilience. When you experience failure, you're forced to pick yourself up and try again. This can be a difficult and uncomfortable process, but it also allows you to develop a sense of strength and perseverance that can be applied to all areas of your life.

In addition to resilience, failure can also help you to develop a growth mindset. A growth mindset is the belief that your abilities and intelligence can be developed through hard work, effort, and dedication. When you experience failure, you're forced to reassess your approach and try new strategies. This can help you to develop a growth mindset, as you learn to see failure as an opportunity for growth and improvement rather than a reflection of your abilities.

Another reason why failure is valuable is that it can help you to develop empathy and understanding for others. When you experience failure, you become more aware of the struggles and challenges that others may be facing. This can help you to become more compassionate and understanding, which can be an asset in the workplace. By learning from your own failures, you can become more sensitive to the struggles of others, and you can become a more effective team player.

Of course, it's important to note that failure doesn't always lead to success. Sometimes, despite your best efforts, you may still fail to achieve your goals. However, even in these situations, there are still valuable lessons to be learned. For example, failure can help you to develop a greater sense of humility and appreciation for the hard work of others. It can also help you to identify areas where you need to improve and develop a more realistic understanding of your strengths and weaknesses.

So, if failure is such a valuable learning experience, why do so many people fear it? One reason is that failure is often associated with shame and embarrassment. When you fail, you may feel like you've let yourself and others down. However, it's important to remember that failure is not a reflection of your worth as a person. Instead, it's a natural part of the learning process that can help you to grow and develop.

Another reason why people fear failure is that they worry about the consequences. In the workplace, failure can sometimes lead to negative consequences such as job loss or damage to your reputation. However, it's important to remember that failure is not always a catastrophic event. In fact, many organizations encourage risk-taking and innovation, recognizing that failure is often a necessary step on the path to success.

So, how can you learn to embrace failure and use it as a learning opportunity? Here are a few tips:

1. **Reframe failure as a learning opportunity**. Instead of viewing failure as a negative experience, try to see it as a chance to learn and grow.

2. **Cultivate a growth mindset**. Focus on the belief that your abilities and intelligence can be developed through hard work, effort, and dedication.

3. **Surround yourself with supportive people**. Having a supportive network can help you to see failure in a

different light and encourage you to keep pushing forward.

4. **Analyse and reflect on your failures**. Take the time to analyse what went wrong and what you could have done differently. This can help you to avoid making the same mistakes in the future.

5. **Take calculated risks**. While failure is often necessary for growth, it's important to take calculated risks rather than reckless ones. Consider the potential consequences before taking action.

6. **Practice self-compassion**. Don't be too hard on yourself when you fail. Remember that everyone fails at some point, and it's important to treat yourself with kindness and understanding.

7. **Set realistic goals**. Setting goals that are too high can set you up for failure. Make sure your goals are challenging but attainable, and celebrate small successes along the way. Remember that failure is not the end of the world. It's a natural part of the learning and growth process. By reframing your mindset and embracing failure as an opportunity to learn and grow, you can overcome your fear of failure and achieve your goals.

In conclusion, failure is not something to be feared, but rather a valuable opportunity for growth and learning. By shifting our mindset and reframing our perspective on failure, we can turn it into a stepping stone towards success.

It's important to remember that success is not measured by the absence of failure, but rather by the ability to learn from it and keep moving forward. So, embrace failure, take calculated risks, surround yourself with supportive people, and always remember to be kind to yourself along the way. With these tools, you'll be well on your way to achieving your goals and realizing your full potential.

The Benefits of Exercise at Work: How Physical Activity Can Improve Your Workday

Physical exercise is essential for maintaining good health and wellness. However, many people spend a significant portion of their day sitting at a desk, which can have negative effects on their health. Studies have shown that incorporating exercise into your workday can have significant benefits for both your physical and mental health, as well as improving productivity and job satisfaction.

One of the primary benefits of exercise at work is that it can help combat the negative effects of prolonged sitting. Sitting for extended periods of time has been linked to increased risks of obesity, heart disease, diabetes, and other chronic health conditions. However, even a brief amount of physical activity during the workday can help mitigate these risks. Studies have shown that taking just a 10-minute walk during the workday can improve mood, reduce fatigue, and increase overall energy levels.

Another benefit of exercise at work is that it can improve productivity. Studies have found that employees who exercise regularly are more productive and efficient in their work. Exercise has been shown to increase focus, cognitive function, and creativity, which can lead to better problem-solving skills and more innovative thinking. Regular exercise has also been linked to better sleep quality, which can further improve work performance.

In addition to physical benefits, exercise at work can also have significant mental health benefits. Exercise has been shown to reduce stress and anxiety, which are common in the workplace. It can also help improve mood and self-esteem, leading to increased job satisfaction and overall well-being.

There are many ways to incorporate exercise into your workday, even if you have a sedentary job. One option is to take regular breaks to stretch, walk, or do some simple exercises at your desk. There are many exercises you can do while seated, such as leg lifts, calf raises, and desk push-ups. You can also take the stairs instead of the elevator, park farther away from your building to increase your walking distance, or take a walk during your lunch break.

Another option is to participate in workplace wellness programs. Many employers offer wellness programs that include exercise classes, gym memberships, and other activities to help employees stay active and healthy. These programs can be a great way to incorporate exercise into your workday and meet other like-minded colleagues.

It is important to remember that exercise at work should be enjoyable and sustainable. It is easy to get discouraged or feel overwhelmed if you try to take on too much at once. Start with small, manageable goals and build from there. Remember to listen to your body and take breaks when you need them.

In conclusion, there are many benefits to incorporating exercise into your workday. Physical activity can help combat the negative effects of prolonged sitting, improve productivity and job satisfaction, and have significant mental health benefits. There are many ways to incorporate exercise into your workday, and it is important to find an approach that is sustainable and enjoyable for you. By prioritizing exercise and taking care of your physical and mental health, you can set yourself up for success in both your professional and personal life.

Why You Shouldn't Be Afraid to Ask for Help: The Power of Collaboration

In today's fast-paced work environment, it can be easy to feel like you have to tackle everything on your own. There's often a lot of pressure to prove your worth and show that you can handle any task or project that comes your way. However, this mentality can lead to burnout, stress, and ultimately, a decrease in productivity. This is where the power of collaboration comes in. In this article, we'll explore why you shouldn't be afraid to ask for help and how working together can benefit both you and your team.

First, let's examine why people may be hesitant to ask for help in the first place. One reason may be fear of appearing incompetent or weak. Many people feel like they should be able to handle everything on their own, and asking for help may seem like a sign of weakness. Others may worry about burdening their colleagues with extra work or worry that they will be seen as lazy if they ask for assistance.

However, the truth is that asking for help is a sign of strength, not weakness. It shows that you are aware of your limitations and are willing to seek out solutions to overcome them. It also shows that you value the input and expertise of your colleagues and are committed to working together to achieve a common goal.

Collaboration can benefit everyone involved in a number of ways. For one, it allows team members to share their unique perspectives and skills. When different people with different backgrounds and areas of expertise come together to solve a problem, they are able to approach it from multiple angles, which can lead to more creative and effective solutions. Additionally, working together can help build trust and strengthen relationships within the team.

Another benefit of collaboration is that it can help alleviate stress and prevent burnout. When one person is solely responsible for a project or task, it can be overwhelming and lead to feelings of anxiety or frustration. However, when team members work together, the workload is shared, and everyone can pitch in to help. This can help prevent burnout and ensure that everyone is able to maintain a healthy work-life balance.

Collaboration can also lead to professional growth and development. When you work with others, you have the opportunity to learn from their experiences and gain new skills. Additionally, working on a project with a team can help you develop important soft skills like communication, leadership, and problem-solving.

So how can you start embracing collaboration and asking for help when you need it? Here are a few tips:

1. **Recognize your limitations**. It's important to be aware of your strengths and weaknesses and acknowledge when you need assistance. This can help you avoid taking on too much and ultimately burning out.

2. **Be clear about what you need**. When asking for help, be specific about what you need assistance with and what you hope to achieve. This can help your colleagues understand how they can best support you.

3. **Be willing to reciprocate**. Collaboration is a two-way street. If you ask for help, be prepared to offer assistance when your colleagues need it as well.

4. **Foster open communication**. Create an environment where team members feel comfortable sharing their thoughts and ideas. This can help encourage collaboration and ensure that everyone feels valued.

In conclusion, collaboration is a powerful tool that can benefit both individuals and teams. By embracing collaboration and asking for help when you need it, you can alleviate stress, build stronger relationships with your colleagues, and ultimately achieve greater success in the workplace. Remember, asking for help is a sign of strength, not weakness. So don't be afraid to reach out and work together with your colleagues to achieve your goals.

The Secret to Success: The Importance of Persistence in the Workplace

Persistence is often seen as the key ingredient to success in the workplace. It's the ability to keep going, even when things get tough. It's the determination to overcome obstacles and to continue striving towards a goal. It's what separates those who achieve great things from those who give up too easily. In this article, we will explore the importance of persistence in the workplace and how it can help you achieve your goals.

What is Persistence?

Persistence is an essential trait that is required in all aspects of life, not just the workplace. It is the key to achieving success and overcoming the obstacles that come our way. When we are persistent in our pursuits, we are more likely to achieve our goals and objectives, no matter how challenging they may seem.

In the workplace, persistence is particularly important. It is often the difference between a successful employee and a mediocre one. Persistent employees are those who keep going, even when faced with obstacles, setbacks, or failures. They have the determination to achieve their goals and the tenacity to keep working towards them, no matter what.

Persistent employees are also more likely to be resilient. When faced with challenges, they are able to bounce back quickly and find new solutions. They are not deterred by failures or setbacks, but rather use them as learning opportunities. They are constantly improving themselves and their work, and are not afraid to ask for help or advice when needed.

Moreover, persistent employees are more likely to be self-motivated. They do not need external motivation or rewards to keep them going, but rather are driven by their internal desire to achieve their goals. They are able to stay focused and productive even when faced with distractions or competing priorities.

It is important to note that persistence is not the same as stubbornness. While persistence requires a strong sense of determination and perseverance, it also requires the ability to adapt and be flexible when necessary. Persistent employees are able to assess their situation and adjust their approach accordingly, without losing sight of their goals.

In conclusion, persistence is a crucial trait in the workplace. It allows employees to persevere through challenges, meet deadlines, and achieve their goals. It is the difference between success and failure, and separates the average from the exceptional. Persistent employees are resilient, self-motivated, and adaptable, and possess the determination to achieve their objectives no matter what obstacles they may face. By cultivating persistence in the workplace, individuals can set themselves up for long-term success and fulfilment.

Why is Persistence Important in the Workplace?

Persistence is a crucial trait that can help individuals achieve their goals and overcome obstacles in the workplace. There are several reasons why persistence is important in the workplace, including achieving goals, developing resilience, building confidence, enhancing creativity, and improving motivation. These benefits highlight the importance of persistence for personal and professional growth.

One of the most significant benefits of persistence is achieving goals. Persistence enables individuals to keep pushing towards their objectives, even when obstacles and challenges arise. When individuals are persistent, they have the determination to keep working towards their goals, regardless of setbacks or failures. This ability to persevere through challenges can help individuals achieve success in their personal and professional lives.

Another important benefit of persistence is developing resilience. When individuals are persistent, they learn to bounce back from setbacks and failures. Instead of giving up, individuals who are persistent view setbacks as opportunities to learn and grow. This mindset can help individuals become more resilient and better equipped to handle challenges in the workplace.

Persistence can also help individuals build confidence. When individuals achieve their goals through persistence, it can be a huge confidence booster. The more individuals persist, the more they will believe in their ability to overcome obstacles and achieve success. This confidence can spill over into other areas of their lives, including personal relationships and hobbies.

In addition to building confidence, persistence can also enhance creativity. When individuals are persistent, they are more likely to come up with creative solutions to problems. They are not content to accept the first solution that comes to mind. Instead, they keep working on the problem until they find a unique and innovative solution. This creativity can be an asset in the workplace, leading to more innovative ideas and better solutions.

Finally, persistence is important for improving motivation. When individuals are persistent, they are more likely to stay motivated even when things get tough. This motivation can help individuals stay focused on their goals and achieve success. By persisting through challenges and setbacks, individuals can maintain their motivation and drive to achieve their goals.

In conclusion, persistence is a crucial trait for success in the workplace. It enables individuals to achieve their goals, develop resilience, build confidence, enhance creativity, and improve motivation. These benefits demonstrate the importance of persistence for personal and professional growth. By cultivating persistence in the workplace, individuals can overcome challenges and achieve success in their careers.

How to Develop Persistence in the Workplace

Developing persistence is not always easy, but it is possible. Here are some tips for developing persistence in the workplace:

Set Realistic Goals

Setting realistic goals is crucial in developing persistence. Goals that are too ambitious may seem overwhelming and can quickly become demotivating, leading to a decrease in persistence. Conversely, setting goals that are challenging but achievable can help to maintain motivation and boost confidence. It's important to break down larger goals into smaller, more manageable steps to make progress feel attainable. Celebrating small victories along the way can also provide a sense of accomplishment and increase the drive to continue pursuing the larger goal. When goals are realistic, persistence becomes easier to develop and maintain, as progress towards the goal can be seen and celebrated, providing the motivation to push forward.

Break Goals Down into Smaller Steps

To achieve your goals and develop persistence, it's crucial to break them down into smaller, manageable steps. This approach not only helps to track progress but also keeps you motivated by making your goals seem more attainable. Smaller steps can be tackled more easily, providing a sense of accomplishment and momentum towards achieving the ultimate objective. By focusing on these smaller steps, you can also identify potential obstacles or challenges that may arise, allowing you to develop strategies to overcome them before they derail your progress. Breaking down

151

your goals into smaller steps also helps you to stay focused and avoid feeling overwhelmed, as it provides a clear roadmap to follow. Ultimately, this approach allows you to build momentum towards your goal, increasing your chances of success while developing the persistence needed to overcome obstacles and challenges along the way.

Learn from Setbacks

Encountering setbacks and failures is an inevitable part of any professional journey. However, it is crucial to view these challenges as opportunities for growth, rather than letting them defeat you. When you face a setback, take the time to analyse what went wrong, and how you can improve your approach. This kind of introspection will help you learn from your mistakes, and develop new strategies for overcoming future obstacles. It's important to take a step back, assess the situation objectively, and identify areas for improvement. With persistence and a willingness to learn, you can turn setbacks into stepping stones towards success. Remember, setbacks are a natural part of the journey towards achieving your goals, and each setback can provide you with valuable insights and lessons that will help you succeed in the long run. By adopting a growth mindset and viewing challenges as opportunities, you can become a more resilient, determined and ultimately successful individual.

Celebrate Small Wins

Recognizing and celebrating small wins is an effective way to maintain motivation and persistence. Celebrating small achievements helps to create positive emotions and reinforces the idea that progress is being made. Taking time to celebrate these milestones can help to keep you focused and motivated to achieve your larger goal. It's important to recognize that every step forward, no matter how small, is a step closer to achieving your ultimate objective. Celebrating small wins doesn't have to be a big event; it can be as simple as treating yourself to your favourite snack or taking a short break to relax. Celebrating these small successes will not only help you stay motivated but also build confidence and self-belief in your ability to achieve your goals.

Find a Support System

Developing persistence requires effort and support. Having a support system, such as friends, colleagues, or family members, can be beneficial in this journey. Having people who can offer words of encouragement or a listening ear can help you stay motivated, especially during challenging times. Colleagues can offer support by sharing their own experiences or tips on how to deal with setbacks. Friends and family members can also offer a different perspective or provide a much-needed break from work. It is essential to surround yourself with individuals who will uplift and support you, especially when facing difficulties in achieving your goals. It is equally important to reciprocate support and encouragement to your support system when they need it. By creating a positive and supportive environment, you can develop the resilience and determination needed to persist in the face of obstacles.

Practice Patience

Developing persistence is a gradual and continuous process that requires dedication and hard work. It is vital to understand that patience and self-compassion are essential components of this journey. It's easy to get frustrated and disheartened when progress seems slow, but it's important to remind oneself that persistence is not an overnight accomplishment. As with any skill, it takes time, effort, and consistency to master.

It's important to remember that setbacks and obstacles are a natural part of the process. These challenges help to strengthen our resilience and develop our perseverance. Rather than becoming discouraged, it's crucial to maintain a positive outlook and focus on our goals. Every obstacle is an opportunity to learn and grow, so don't be afraid to embrace the difficulties that arise.

Embrace Continuous Learning

The world is constantly changing and evolving, and the workplace is no exception. To stay relevant and successful in your career, it's important to embrace continuous learning. This means seeking out new knowledge and skills that can help you excel in your current role or prepare you for future opportunities.

Fortunately, there are many ways to continue learning throughout your career. You can take courses, attend conferences or seminars, read industry publications, and network with professionals in your field. You can also seek out mentorship and coaching from more experienced colleagues, or join professional associations or groups that offer educational resources and opportunities.

The benefits of continuous learning are numerous. It can help you stay up-to-date with industry trends and advancements, improve your performance and productivity, and increase your confidence and credibility. It can also open up new opportunities for career growth and advancement.

Practice Gratitude

In a fast-paced and competitive work environment, it's easy to focus on the negatives and overlook the positives. However, practicing gratitude can have a powerful impact on your well-being and success.

Gratitude involves focusing on and appreciating the good things in your life, rather than dwelling on the bad. In the workplace, this can mean expressing appreciation for your colleagues, recognizing and celebrating successes, and finding joy and fulfilment in your work.

Research has shown that practicing gratitude can lead to improved physical and mental health, increased resilience, and greater happiness and life satisfaction. It can also help you build stronger relationships with your colleagues and contribute to a more positive work culture.

Set Boundaries

While it's important to be dedicated and committed to your work, it's also important to set boundaries to protect your well-being and prevent burnout. This means establishing clear guidelines and expectations for your work schedule, workload, and communication with colleagues.

Setting boundaries can involve establishing specific working hours, limiting after-hours work communication, and delegating tasks when necessary. It can also mean taking breaks throughout the day, prioritizing self-care and personal time, and saying no to tasks or responsibilities that exceed your capacity.

By setting boundaries, you can avoid becoming overwhelmed and exhausted, and maintain a healthy work-life balance. This, in turn, can help you remain focused and productive in your work and contribute to a more positive work environment.

Celebrate Successes

Finally, it's important to celebrate your successes and those of your colleagues. Celebrating successes can help build morale, foster a sense of community and shared purpose, and motivate individuals to continue striving for excellence.

Celebrating successes can involve recognizing individual achievements through awards or public recognition, as well as celebrating team accomplishments through shared experiences such as team outings or celebrations.

By celebrating successes, you can create a more positive and supportive work culture that values hard work and dedication. This, in turn, can help to build a stronger sense of community and motivation among your colleagues and contribute to your overall success and well-being in the workplace.

Congratulations on finishing this book! You've learned a lot about how to be more productive, efficient, and successful in the workplace. But the real question is, what are you going to do with all of this newfound knowledge? Are you going to let it go in one ear and out the other, or are you going to take action?

The purpose of this book is not just to entertain you with amusing anecdotes or to provide you with theoretical concepts. Its purpose is to inspire you to make changes in your work habits and to give you practical strategies to help you achieve your goals.

So, let's start with the basics. You spend a large portion of your life at work. Whether you love your job or hate it, there's no denying that it has a significant impact on your life. So why not make the most of it? By implementing the tips and tricks outlined in this book, you can increase your productivity, reduce your stress, and achieve your goals.

Start by focusing on the things that matter. Stop wasting your time on unimportant tasks, and instead, prioritize the things that will move you closer to your goals. Remember, multitasking is overrated. By focusing on one task at a time, you'll be able to complete it more quickly and with better quality.

Next, don't be afraid to ask for help. Collaboration is a powerful tool, and by working together, you can achieve more than you ever could on your own. Additionally, be open to feedback and constructive criticism. This is how you grow and improve.

Be assertive, but not aggressive. Stand up for yourself and your ideas, but do so in a way that is respectful and professional. And always be willing to learn. The world is constantly changing, and you need to keep up with the latest trends and technologies to stay ahead.

Finally, remember that persistence is key. You will face obstacles and setbacks, but it's how you handle them that matters. Don't let fear of failure hold you back. Instead, embrace it as an opportunity to learn and grow.

In conclusion, this book has provided you with a wealth of information and strategies to help you succeed in the workplace. But it's up to you to take action. So go out there and put these ideas into practice. Don't wait for tomorrow, do it today! Remember, the secret to success is persistence. Keep working hard, stay focused, and never give up on your dreams.

www.ingramcontent.com/pod-product-compliance
Lightning Source LLC
Chambersburg PA
CBHW070547220526
45467CB00003B/1106